YOU MAKE A DIFFERENCE

BY MICHAEL KELLY

THE EMPIRE
PUBLISHERS

12808 West Airport Blvd Suite 270M Sugar Land, TX 77478, Unites States

https://www.theempirepublishers.com/

Our books may be purchased in bulk for promotional, educational, or business use.

Please contact The Empire Publishers at +1 844 636-4579, or by email at support@theempirepublishers.com

First Edition December 2025

About The Author:

Michael P. Kelly

Retired Public School

Administrator, Teacher, Coach

Michael Kelly earned his Bachelor of Arts in Teaching from Sam Houston State University in 1983, completing the university's coaching emphasis program. That same year, he received the Joe Kirk Award as the Outstanding Kinesiology Student. In 1987, Michael went on to earn a Master of Science in Public School Administration from Texas A&M University–Kingsville.

Michael is Texas certified and has successfully taught a wide range of subjects, including Government, Economics, U.S. History, Texas History, World Geography, World History, Psychology, Sociology, and Physical Education.

Throughout his career, he has served in various roles across several Texas school districts, including Safety Director, Athletic Director, Assistant Principal, Teacher, and Coach. His coaching tenure spans over a decade, with 10 years as a Head Football Coach, 8 years as a Head Track Coach, and 10 years as Head Cross Country and Distance Coach. He has also contributed as an Assistant Coach in Football, Track, and Baseball. His leadership has led to notable achievements, including multiple district and bi-district championships, state playoff appearances, and even a few individual state champions.

As an administrator, Michael made a significant impact. As Athletic Director, he played a key role in launching new programs such as softball, golf, and tennis. Under his leadership, athletic teams achieved 21 championship banners and numerous deep playoff runs. As Safety Director, he successfully transitioned the district's Accident and Workers' Compensation program into a Self-Insured model. While serving as Assistant Principal, he created and implemented the "Increase the Peace" initiative: a discipline and conflict resolution program that was presented at the 2001 North Texas Association of Secondary Principals Conference, where it received wide praise.

Acknowledgments

This book, a collection of thoughts, illustrations, and lived experiences, represents the insights I've gathered over the course of a 35-year journey in education. I've had the privilege of serving in various roles, teacher, coach, and administrator, across several school districts. These roles afforded me both challenges and meaningful successes, and the reflections you'll find in the chapters ahead are rooted in a system of development and growth cultivated within the sphere of our collective influence.

Throughout my career, I've been fortunate to learn from and work alongside many remarkable individuals. While the list is far too long to name everyone, I would like to acknowledge a few who have had a profound impact on my path. Among the outstanding athletic directors and head football coaches whose work and wisdom shaped my own were Gordon Wood, Joe Clements, Roger Tedford, Cynda Baer, Bill Farrah, Jack Robbins, Dan Schreiber, Bob Alpert, Jay Witt, and Eric Ezar. Their legacies include 14 State Championships, numerous playoff victories, and an impressive array of Bi-District and District titles.

I also wish to thank a group of dedicated administrators and coaches who not only valued my contributions but also helped elevate them. I am deeply grateful to Pat West, Linda Opitz, Cynda Baer, Mike O'Bryan, David Poggensee, Bear Guinard, Ralph Harvey, Mark Ruiz, and Bill James for their support and encouragement throughout the years.

My journey began in the early 1980s with a group of fellow graduate students and aspiring administrators. Together, we shared a vision to instill leadership, discipline, and purpose in the lives of the young men and women we were entrusted to guide. We believed in raising expectations and helping students reshape their cultural norms toward excellence. I am especially thankful to Mike O'Bryan, Danny Solis, Dwayne Gerlich, and Jerry Gonzalez for their lasting camaraderie and shared commitment to this work.

To my wife, Shirley, thank you for being the unwavering rock that held our family together during long days and late nights dedicated to serving others. Your strength and grace have made everything possible. To my two daughters, thank you for sharing your father with thousands of students and athletes. I know it wasn't always easy, but your understanding and love mean more than words can express. I am endlessly proud of you both and eternally grateful.

Table of Contents

AGENT OF CHANGE

Change Relies On Ownership Of The Process

Effective leaders understand the value of every staff member, student, and athlete. Each person brings unique traits, expectations, and opportunities for growth. When building a team or organization, it's important to recognize and embrace these differences. The greater the diversity of ideas and perspectives, the easier it is to foster collaboration and engagement.

True leadership involves giving others a stake in the process. When people feel ownership, they become more invested in the outcome, and that's where meaningful success begins.

We are different
but together we make
the world a beautiful place

Evaluating The Culture

When stepping into a new program, one of my first priorities is to assess and reshape the existing culture. This is no easy task. In most cases, staff and participants are entrenched in long-standing attitudes, often negative or resigned. As a leader, your mission is to shift these perceptions by promoting positivity, reinforcing a sense of purpose, and setting high expectations.

You must paint a vision of what success looks like, then help others see it for themselves. By consistently doing the right things and modeling strong values, you can show people that their actions and attitudes do influence the direction of their lives.

You can't change a person who doesn't see an issue in their actions.

Have A Clear Vision

One of the greatest challenges in leading cultural change is dealing with narrow-minded individuals, those who make excuses and cling to negativity. As a leader, you must be the motivator, the encourager, and the example. With faith, resilience, and unwavering determination, stay focused and optimistic.

Start small. Establish achievable goals that lay the foundation for your broader vision. Then create a clear, actionable roadmap. Provide direction and lead by example, every day. Talk less, lead more.

People who say it cannot be done should not interrupt those who are doing it.

Share The Vision

This is my motto whenever I step into a new role: **Why settle, when the possibilities are endless?** As a leader, it's your job to set meaningful goals and establish incentives that inspire staff and students. Help them believe there's something greater ahead.

The vision begins with your core team. From there, it spreads with enthusiasm. True progress comes when participants buy in, uniting behind a common purpose to move forward together.

We cannot become what we want by remaining what we are.

Your Vision Leads Your Preparation

This is why you were chosen to lead. Your experience, insight, and commitment are essential. Success doesn't happen by chance: it requires vision, preparation, and follow-through. When your hard work meets opportunity, be ready to seize it.

People may call it "luck," but more often than not, it's destiny shaped by determination. Early on, critics may doubt the path forward, but when progress becomes visible, even skeptics turn into supporters. Stay the course. Keep leading. Others will follow.

It's not that I can't see what they see
It's that I see what they can't.

Real Change

One of my favorite illustrations is about the difference between temporary fixes and lasting change. As a young teacher or coach, understand this: there are no shortcuts when it comes to real impact. Working with students means investing in their futures.

Real change demands hard work, high standards, strong role models, consistent encouragement, and a clear vision. When you lead with conviction and integrity, you can instill confidence and shape lasting outcomes. The impression you make today will echo far beyond the classroom or the field.

What comes easy won't last, what lasts won't come easy.

Lean On Your Self Confidence In The Beginning

As an educational leader, I often found myself leading from the front. Many people are natural followers, they want or need someone to guide them, but before they commit, they'll evaluate your objectives and question your motives. Then there are the self-starters. These individuals don't necessarily need leadership, but they do need to be convinced and inspired. In the beginning, expect to walk alone. Trust your vision, stay confident and committed, and over time, everything will begin to align

.

Consistency is harder when no one is clapping for you. You must clap for yourself during these times; you should always be your biggest fan.

Don't Hesitate, Don't Wait

In my career as both a coach and administrator, I was often hired to be the agent of change. Schools and programs sought me out for my ability to shift mindsets, raise expectations, and deliver results. The first few weeks are critical: filled with introductions, evaluations, and strategic planning. Get to know the people, understand their influence, and define their roles. Don't hesitate, and certainly don't wait. Change doesn't come to those who delay.

Water ain't gonna clear up until you get the pigs outta the creek!

9

Move In A Confident Direction

When tasked with improving a school or athletic program, it's vital to remember: this is not a popularity contest. You must move forward with confidence and clarity of purpose. Some will follow eagerly. Others will resist change because they're content with the status quo. And then there will be those who oppose you out of envy or insecurity. As a leader, you must stay focused, remain steady, and push everyone toward progress.

Confidence is not: "They will like me."

Confidence is: "I'll be fine if they don't."

Accept The Challenge

To accept a challenge is to boldly confront what lies ahead. As educators, we face challenges daily, and we're being watched in how we respond. Approach each one with patience, integrity, determination, and strength. Never lead with intimidation or anger. Instead, let your inner spirit and faith guide your response. In doing so, you not only overcome the obstacle, you earn trust and respect.

A challenge: You can either be afraid of it or excited about it. You can either attack it or run from it.

Command Respect

If you've ever worked with me, whether as a student, teacher, coach, or administrator, you likely formed a strong opinion of me from the start. You either loved me or didn't. But over time, through shared hard work, dedication, and mutual effort, we came to understand one another. I never aimed to be popular or to be your friend, but I did demand your respect, and I always gave you mine in return. I made it a point to praise, encourage, and challenge those around me. In the end, we parted ways with a sense of shared respect and pride in our journey. I am forever grateful to the staff, students, and families I've been privileged to work with.

Your journey is not the same as mine, and my journey is not yours, but if we meet on a certain path, may we encourage each other.

KEYS TO PROGRESS

Exemplify A Presence

I've always believed a great teacher or coach should be able to command a room. I had that gift: the ability to walk in, earn attention, deliver a message, and end with a prayer of thanks. I didn't always understand where that confidence came from. But as I matured, both professionally and spiritually, I recognized it as a blessing from God.

As a child, I struggled with stuttering. It was difficult and deeply embarrassing. But through relentless determination and countless prayers, I overcame it. By high school, I had become the captain of my football team and a leader in my church youth group. I accepted Jesus into my life at age 15 and was baptized. From that moment, I knew the light inside me was meant to shine, especially in moments of challenge. I give God full credit for guiding me, strengthening me, and allowing others to see that light in classrooms, on fields, in auditoriums, and in gymnasiums. It's a gift, and I am blessed.

The brighter the light, the darker the shadow.

-Carl Jung

Have Urgency

When you're brought in to lead change, time is not on your side. I learned early on that urgency is essential. If a school or program is struggling, change must begin immediately. Evaluation and planning are crucial, but they must be done quickly and strategically. There's generally a 3–5-year window to show real improvement.

And be warned: success doesn't always bring support. When you disrupt the status quo, you'll make waves. Some people will never appreciate or accept you: no matter the results. Even as your programs improve, opposition will often grow. By year five, you may find yourself working on borrowed time. This is a reality many superintendents, principals, and head coaches know well. It's not pessimism, it's the nature of transformational leadership, and it's supported by experience and research.

Everyone isn't proud of you. They're just surprised you keep making things happen.

Don't Wait, Take The Initiative

As an agent of change and an effective leader, you must be ready to take initiative from day one. Your approach must be confident, deliberate, and inspiring. When stepping into a new role, understand that you are in a brief honeymoon period, typically just 5 to 6 months. During this time, people will be open to your ideas, giving you the latitude to set a new direction, shift expectations, and reshape attitudes. Use this window wisely. Push your vision forward without hesitation, because time is limited, and critics will eventually emerge.

Initiative built on a defined understanding of what must be achieved puts one in harmony with everyone around him, and with the universe as a whole.

Be Diligent

This message serves as a powerful reminder: your effort matters. Even when it's unclear whether your words or actions are being noticed, know that positive reinforcement and goodwill always leave an impression. In the end, it's your attitude and consistent effort that define your legacy. Strive daily to be the best version of yourself.

You may not always see the results of your kindness... but every bit of positive energy you contribute to the world makes it a better place for all of us.

Don't Be Distracted

Obstacles and adversity are inevitable parts of leadership. Some challenges you can predict with keen observation and preparation. Others will arrive without warning, and when they do, they may feel overwhelming. In those moments, pause. A deep breath, a quiet prayer, or a moment of silence can ground your emotions and restore your clarity. More often than not, what felt like a crisis one day seems far less significant the next.

Press on. Obstacles are seldom the same size tomorrow as they are today.

-Robert H. Schuller

Stay The Course, Keep Moving Forward

When tasked with turning around a struggling program, you must remain laser-focused on the immediate needs of your staff and participants. As the catalyst for change, you're called to be part salesperson, part disciplinarian, and a consistent model of character and leadership. Expect resistance. Expect distractions. But wear your blinders and lead with purpose. Others will follow when they see your unwavering focus. Never look back. Just keep moving forward.

Successful people never worry about what others are doing.

Stay True To Your Belief System

To every young coach and educator: stay grounded in your values. Your experiences are only meaningful if they reinforce the foundation you stand on. Know who you are. Trust your intuition. Listen to your inner voice. These qualities will guide you through challenges and help you stay aligned with your purpose and goals.

Be like a tree.
Stay grounded.
Connect with your roots.
Turn over a new leaf.
Bend before you break.
Enjoy your unique natural beauty.
Keep growing.

-Joanne Raptis

Preparation And Effort

Peyton Manning, a Hall of Fame quarterback respected across the NFL, spoke often about the power of preparation. His success wasn't just natural talent; it was built on relentless practice and maximum effort. He reminded us that peak performance is found at the intersection of preparation and effort. Adopt this mindset, and greatness will follow.

I never left the field saying 'I could have done more to get ready' and that gives me peace of mind.

-Peyton Manning.

Building Strength And Teamwork

In the early stages of building a program, expect adversity. Losses may pile up, morale may dip, and doubt may creep in. But as the leader, you must remain steady and encouraging. Rally your team. Inspire them. Many great leaders live by the mantra: "It's us against the world." Everyone must pull together, hold the rope tightly, and climb that mountain, together. Believe that the light at the end of the tunnel is real, even when it feels far away.

We still have faith and we have each other, so let's stay strong!

-Mark Wahlberg

Know Your Participants, Build Relationships

Creating change also means connecting with people. A teacher or coach must be able to build strong, meaningful relationships with their team. A good leader facilitates conversations that spark growth, self-awareness, and progress. Establish trust. Communicate clearly. Foster accountability and a culture of continuous learning. When done right, your team will not only respect your leadership, they'll seek it. They'll want to be coached by you.

Everyone wants to be coached, you just have to find the right way to reach them.

-Chuck Daily

No Limitations, No Excuses

As a teacher and coach, I always believed that every effort counts. I taught my participants that we live in the greatest country in the world, where opportunities for success are right in front of us. My challenge to each of them was to discover their passion and pursue it with diligence and commitment. I wanted them to understand that limitations are often just excuses. Anything is possible if you want it badly enough. My hope for all of them has always been a lifetime of purpose and fulfillment.

What you do makes a difference, and you have to decide what kind of difference you want to make.

Focus On The Finish Line

This message echoed in every classroom and on every field under my leadership. In every in-service and interview, I listened closely for signs of this belief. Anyone who has ever worked with me or for me can attest that I was relentless in offering praise, affirmation, and encouragement. These actions illuminate personal achievement and success, for both students and athletes. They are the foundation of our profession.

Our background and circumstances may have influenced who we are, but we are responsible for who we become.

-Barbara Geraci

Professional Attitude

A professional attitude is essential for building a program and ensuring its longevity. The statement below reflects my commitment to culture change and encouraging participants to believe in themselves and each other. If you know me, you know the strength of my will and the persistence behind every step I take.

At the lower frequencies, we are prone to fight the old

At the higher frequencies, we are prone to create the new

What You Say Matters

In academics and athletics, transforming the culture of a school or athletic program is no small task. As the leader, you must set the tone from the front. Your words carry weight, and your narrative should be positive, guiding your team with clarity and high expectations. Understand that your staff and participants are always watching and learning from your example.

People need to learn that their actions do affect other people.

So be careful what you say and do, it's not always just about you.

Give Respect To Get Respect

This simple rule is the bedrock of professional interaction. As a leader, be mindful of your words and actions. When setting expectations or giving directives, ask yourself whether you'd be willing to follow the same. The world may not always be fair, but your treatment of others should always be respectful and just.

Simple rule in life: If you wouldn't like it done to you, don't do it to others.

Utilize Your Strong Will

Those who know me understand how deeply I believe in the power of inner strength. Though I was physically strong as a young coach, I came to value the role of persistent will even more. It shaped my career, helped me through illness, spiritual reflection, and personal loss. That soulful will, I believe, is part of God's design. As it says in *Jeremiah 29:11*: "For I know the plans I have for you… plans to prosper you and not to harm you, plans to give you hope and a future." As a leader, this inner drive was central to establishing expectations and achieving goals.

Strength does not come from physical capacity.

It comes from an indomitable will.

-Mahatma Gandhi

Positive Change Provides Opportunities

It never fails to amaze me how quickly people want to hire someone who brings competence, experience, and results. What they often overlook is the hard work and resolve it takes to change a negative culture. This work isn't for the faint-hearted, insecure, or overly cautious. Once that culture shifts in a positive direction, a good leader continues to monitor, adjust, and evaluate. And eventually, there comes a time when those services are needed elsewhere, where fresh ideas and hard-earned wisdom can take root again.

You can't force anyone to values, respect, understand, or support you, but you can choose to spend your time around people who do.

No Dream Is Too Big

If you knew me well, you knew I always had my eye on the prize. I got my first high school coaching job at the age of 20. I coached inside linebackers at a school near Kelly Air Force Base in San Antonio, Texas. The athletes were exceptional, especially the two inside linebackers, both physically gifted. That talent was a big reason I accepted the job.

During my final interview, the head coach asked me what made me different from other candidates. I told him that while I had been a solid high school and college player, I lacked the natural physical gifts his linebackers had. What I could offer was an attitude and a plan, to help those players become the best in the state. When he asked how I planned to do that, I said, "I'll change their mindset, their knowledge of the game, their drive to be great, and their dreams, to include college football and a quality education." He laughed, then asked when I could start.

Two years later, the older player became a *Parade* All-American, one of only two in the country that year, and earned a full scholarship to SMU, later graduating with a degree in Finance. The following year, the younger player also became a *Parade* All-American and signed with TCU. He remains, to this day, the only high school football player I've coached who could've stepped off a high school field and into the NFL. He was strong, smart, fearless, and read offenses like no one else. He wasn't just good, he was exceptional.

Coaching him was a privilege. Their dreams weren't just big, they were massive. People laughed at my goals in the beginning, but three years later, no one was laughing.

Remember…no dream is too big.

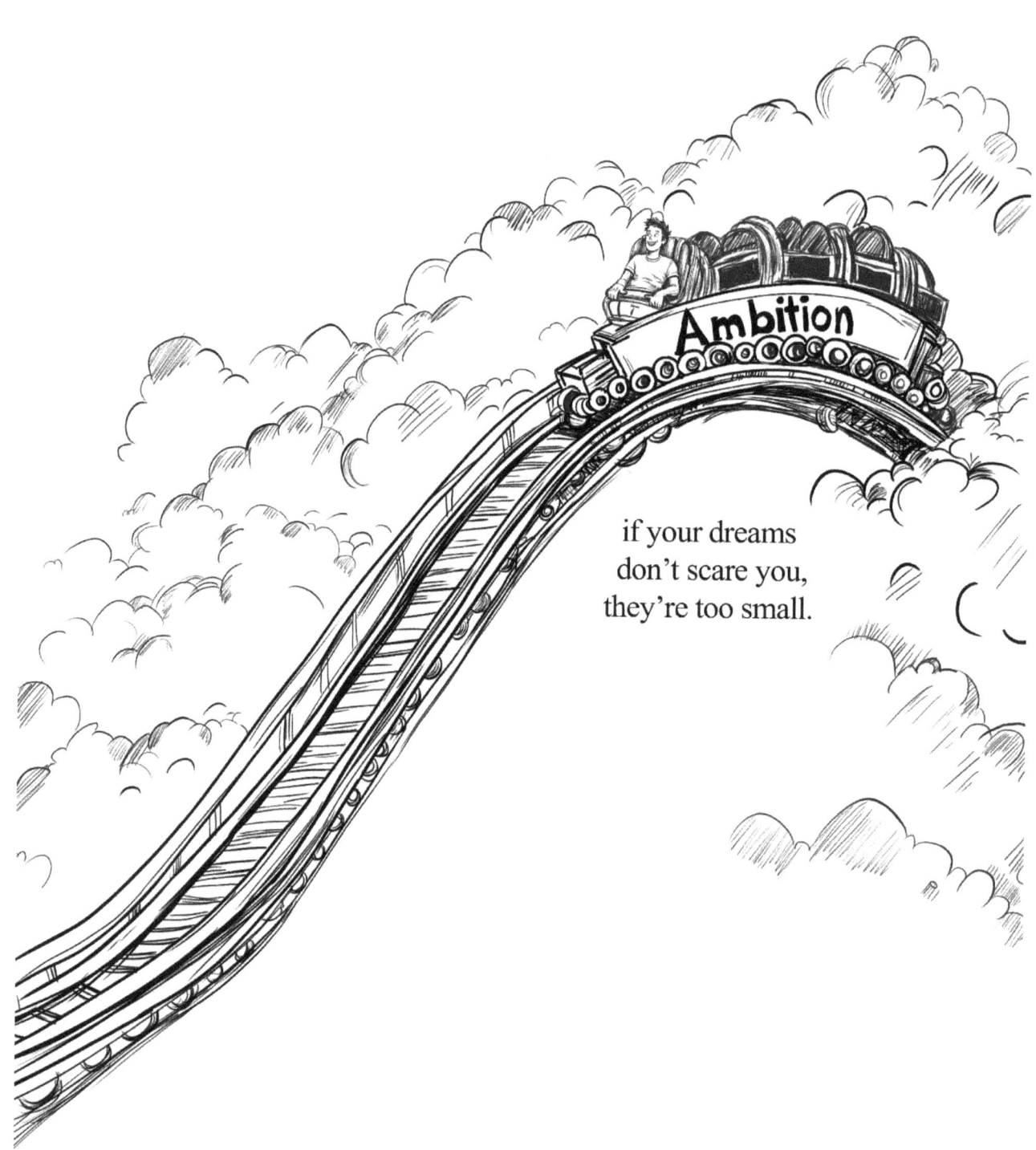

if your dreams
don't scare you,
they're too small.

The Dream Initiates Progress

If you are teaching or coaching kids, you must believe in their potential. If you think your job is only to instill discipline, teach plays and defenses, and give pep talks, then you've missed the bigger picture. Those are important aspects of the job, but your most vital role is to see each child as they truly are: their talent, their knowledge, and their potential.

You should develop a plan for each individual and the team as a whole. After sharing your evaluation with each player, gather the team and encourage them to dream big. Help them define both personal and team goals. Then, work alongside them every day to make steady progress, never losing sight of the ultimate objective.

Some of them will doubt themselves, so you must become a salesman, convincing them of the possibilities. When a shared vision takes hold, it becomes a powerful, unbreakable bond. And when that dream is finally realized, the accomplishment becomes a lifelong memory for everyone involved.

There is a powerful driving force inside every human being that, once unleashed, can make any vision, dream, or desire a reality.

All Things Are Possible

To my former students and athletes, this has always been my message to you. We live in the most opportunistic and promising country in the world. Despite challenges like prejudice or economic barriers, our freedoms and possibilities can be realized through hard work, determination, and willpower.

We all have choices, and one of the best investments you can make is in yourself. Never lose faith, and always stay positive about the direction of your life.

All things are possible, so stop doubting yourself and life. We've all made mistakes, and those mistakes have made us fearful of today and the expectations of tomorrow. You've got to believe because all things are possible. Let's go.

Create A Culture Of Determination

This has always been my mindset. My emphasis was on helping others become the best version of themselves. The culture I believe in is built on hard work, maximum effort, attention to detail, curiosity about your limits, and a constant drive for self-improvement.

Many of my students and athletes can attest to how relentless I was in pushing them toward excellence, academically and athletically. Of course, there were some who didn't get it or didn't want it, and I know I frustrated them. But I suspect that, as they moved into adulthood, they came to understand what I was trying to instill.

A great coach doesn't just accept who and where you are-
they push you to become who you are meant to be so
you can go where you aremeant to go. When your
coach pushes you, pulls you, and holds you
accountable, it's because they see more in
you, and they take their responsibility
to bring it out of you seriously.
It's because they care about
you and your future.

Encourage A Great Work Ethic

Whenever I took over a new program as the educational leader, I would spend time observing and measuring the work ethic of both staff and students. As an agent of change, you only have a small window to instill motivation and help others recognize the value of consistent, maximum effort.

This is an area that can be transformed with clear communication, positive reinforcement, and well-defined goals. You and your team can work together to encourage others and explore possibilities.

I've witnessed remarkable transformations once a group was properly motivated. Changes in work ethic and effort often become permanent, and ultimately serve as lifelong skills.

The goal is to look back one day and say, "Dang, all that hard work was worth it."

Exemplify Courage

Courage is the strength of mind to persevere in the face of difficulty or danger. Not everyone is born with it, but it can be developed.

When I took a head coaching job at a school that had only won two games in ten seasons, my initial evaluation of the program was bleak: no strength, no speed, a poor work ethic, and little positive leadership. That's where we started.

On my first day, I walked out to roll call and saw 100 athletes horsing around. I blew my whistle loudly, got their attention, organized them into lines, and harshly introduced myself. I had them lie on their backs, knees up, and mouths shut. We did crunches on command: elbows to knees, back down, counting in unison.

We started with 50, rested in silence, and during that quiet time, I laid out my expectations. In one hour, they completed 400 crunches and 400 pushups. I told them to come back tomorrow with a new attitude.

The next day, 90 of the 100 returned, completely changed. Those 90 showed me what courage looks like. A few years later, that same group won the first District Championship in the 100-year history of the school district.

Courage doesn't always roar. Sometimes courage is the little voice at the end of the day that says I'll try again tomorrow.

— Mary Anne Radmacher

Facilitate Your Environment

Stephen Hawking was a pretty smart guy. He understood knowledge deeply. Most of us spend a lifetime accumulating facts, experience, and observations. But every once in a while, you'll meet someone who seems to already know it all. These people can be difficult to work with.

In education, you'll meet your fair share of them. I once coached one of the most talented teams in the state, serving as the offensive coordinator and play-caller. During games, I had a coach in the press box tracking the number of touches for our top 18 offensive players. His job was to keep count, because I couldn't. I was always three plays ahead and focused on execution.

At halftime, I reviewed the data and used it to make second-half adjustments. During the second half, I received updates while we were on defense. Why all this effort? Because we had 14 players being recruited for Division I football, and every parent had my cell number, and wasn't afraid to use it.

Those parents believed they knew more than I did. Honestly, some probably thought they had forgotten more about football than I would ever know. But the data helped. The performance chart gave me facts to explain decisions. It was just another tool, one that helped me manage expectations and maintain transparency.

"The greatest enemy of knowledge is not ignorance; it is the illusion of knowledge."

-Stephen Hawking

CHARACTERISTICS OF LEADERSHIP

Competitive Spirit and the Will to Succeed

It's no accident that certain teams and sports programs consistently rise to the top year after year. These programs share some uncommon but powerful traits. They demand discipline, hard work, determination, and genuine development of talent. They believe in setting high expectations and maintaining consistency. They foster growth, both personally and athletically. These programs instill a competitive spirit and the will to win. More importantly, they teach athletes how to overcome adversity and take responsibility for their actions. These qualities are what separate great programs from mediocre or struggling ones.

Scholastics Before Athletics

For over 40 years, the athletes I coached came to understand a simple truth: being part of a successful program meant more than just being a good athlete. I emphasized that their primary reason for coming to school was to learn and grow academically. Good grades and positive classroom behavior were non-negotiable. Teachers and administrators knew they could count on me to enforce that standard. I expected my players to attend class, give their best effort, and aim for academic excellence. And believe me, they did. Many were talented athletes and exceptional teammates. But above all, they understood the expectation to always give their best. There was no room for slackers or "chili dogs" in our program.

There Is No Room for Excuses

Anyone who knows me will tell you: I have no patience for excuses. If you make one, own it, and then work hard to make it right. I don't know a single educator or coach who can tolerate excuse-making. We go above and beyond to help kids learn from their mistakes and move forward. Excuses have no place in the pursuit of excellence. And when you work with young people, don't enable them, hold them accountable. Otherwise, everyone suffers.

Be Fair with the Truth

Know your relationship with the truth. Telling the truth isn't always easy. It can have unexpected consequences. They say the truth will set you free, and that might be true, but it also requires careful judgment. Sometimes, the truth is best shared in private. Sometimes, it's best withheld. Use intuition and common sense to decide. Understand that there can be different perspectives on what the truth is. Your job is to be fair, compassionate, and consistent, while staying devoted to the truth.

A coach can help you with your mistakes, but nobody can help you with your excuses.

-Buzz Williams

Make a Difference

If you're a young teacher or coach, understand this: your role in a child's life is irreplaceable. Once you build a relationship with them, the influence you have can last a lifetime. As the years pass, the memories and lessons you leave behind become more meaningful than you may ever realize. I've seen it firsthand. When former students reconnect with me, there's always a heartfelt hug or handshake, a quick update on life, and sincere gratitude. In retirement, those moments have become more frequent, and deeply rewarding. If you do your job right, these relationships and memories will stay with you forever.

A Passionate Servant

If you met me in a gym or a grocery store, you probably wouldn't know I was a leader of young men and women. My passion and commitment might not be obvious unless you asked, and if you did, be ready, because I'll definitely share! (LOL!) I've led school-wide assemblies, taken teams to Texas Stadium in front of 35,000 fans, and spoken at banquets with 1,500 people in attendance. But I've also comforted students grieving the loss of a loved one, made home visits for those in need, and fed kids who hadn't eaten in days. After a tough loss, I once led our entire field: cheerleaders, pep squad, band, and players, in the most heartfelt Lord's Prayer I've ever heard.

Through it all, I tried to set aside ego and serve as a vessel.

"Do nothing from selfishness or empty conceit, but with humility of mind regard one another as more important than yourselves. Do not merely look out for your own personal interests, but also for the interests of others."

—Philippians 2:3–4

I won't claim I've never struggled with ego, or that I haven't needed to be humbled. I'm human. I've had to ask for forgiveness more than once. But I can say that my spirit and intentions have always been sincere. Those I've served can speak to that. My wife and kids often tell me I'm one of a kind, and I believe that. I know I'm different from the rest.

Humble enough to know that I'm not better than anybody, but wise enough to know that I'm different from the rest.

Be an Influencer

An influencer is someone who has the ability to shape the opinions and behaviors of others by promoting values essential to growth and success. I often refer to myself as an influencer and a catalyst for cultural change within a program. If you're a young teacher or coach, you'll have to decide your role within your program. We all chart our own career paths. I chose to be an influencer, someone who impacts the lives of students and athletes beyond the field or court. Don't get me wrong. Winning and achievement were always important to me. But they never outweighed personal growth, maturity, and the development of lifelong skills.

Encourage a Competitive Spirit, Strong Will, and Determination

Many educators describe certain students or athletes as "winners." Hall of Fame basketball player Larry Bird once said, *"A winner is someone who recognizes his God-given talents, works his tail off to develop them into skills, and uses these skills to accomplish his goals."* My definition of a winner is similar: someone who achieves success through admirable effort and ability. That kind of success stems from a strong competitive spirit, willpower, and determination. Some people are naturally driven, while others develop those traits over time. A good educator knows how to identify both, and how to guide each type toward excellence.

Self-Discipline and Emotional Control

When leading a program in need of a fresh direction, self-discipline and emotional control are essential. Participants are often worn down by negativity but uncertain about change. As the leader, you must model the behavior you expect. People will follow your example if it's rooted in positivity and clarity. I like to start with small things: sportsmanship, encouragement, mutual respect. Many of my former players and students will remember my motto: *"Never let them see you sweat, just do your best."* That principle is highly teachable and helps build poise and resilience. Without emotional control, you leave the door open for opponents and setbacks to get the best of you. A team's success depends heavily on its ability to stay calm and confident under pressure.

Teach Loyalty

As an athletic director, I once worked in a district where doing the right thing often got lost in politics. So, I carefully assembled a team: head and assistant coaches, custodians, field workers, bus drivers, and ticket takers. It took a full year to bring this group together, and I formed a trusted inner circle from within it. Every person I hired understood the value of loyalty and commitment from the start. In a politically charged environment, loyalty and trust became our strongest defense. Many came with the right attitude, and those who didn't learned quickly. We emphasized loyalty during our summer orientation, before the students even arrived. Over the years, this group of over 50 individuals became the tightest-knit team I've ever worked with. Many of us are still close today. Though time and careers have moved on, our mutual respect and connection remain strong.

Never let them see you sweat. When you pout, cuss, kick dirt and throw your helmet, you're sending a message to your opponents and teammates. That you've been beaten.

Emphasize Respect

As an educational leader, I've long recognized the importance of teaching respect to those under my guidance. Respect means acknowledging someone's abilities and worth, and valuing their feelings and perspectives, even when you don't agree. It's about treating others as equals and offering them the same consideration you'd expect for yourself. A simple but powerful gesture of respect is making eye contact when you speak with someone. However, it's important to remember that in some cultures, this may have different meanings. As a young teacher or coach, understanding cultural differences will help you better teach and model respectful behavior within American cultural norms.

Relationships, Preparation, and Caring

There's nothing more fulfilling than seeing the light come on in a student or athlete's eyes when they finally understand a concept or master a skill. If you're a compassionate teacher or coach, remember that every student learns differently. Your goal should be to build trust, discover their learning styles, and adapt your teaching methods to meet their needs. The time and preparation it takes is worth it, always.

I think the most beautiful thing in the world is watching the light come on in someone's eyes, in the dark for so long.

Organization and Work Ethic

Being a head coach requires extraordinary effort and dedication. While most parents, teachers, and administrators focus on the surface, like game strategies and win-loss records, the real work happens beneath, in the unseen hours. Winning is often viewed as the only metric of success, but it's actually the result of countless hours spent managing, planning, and leading, typically 90 to 100 hours a week during the season. For those who believe coaches are overpaid, consider this: when calculated by the hour, the pay averages out to about $2.00 an hour. Coaches don't do it for the money; they do it to help kids grow into confident, committed, and compassionate adults. These life lessons outlast any scoreboard.

Execute the Plan – Enjoy the Ride

I've been blessed to experience incredible moments that many can only dream about. The joy and excitement of success is unmatched. But success isn't accidental, it's the product of a solid plan, unwavering persistence, and high expectations. So have your plan, stick to it, encourage those around you, stay focused, and most importantly, get out of your own way!

Promote a Positive Sphere of Influence

As a professional educator, your influence can extend to teachers, coaches, students, parents, and community members. Your position and commitment create countless opportunities to show compassion, integrity, and care. Trust that these opportunities will come. Just stay spiritually grounded and listen to your inner voice. As **Galatians 6:10** reminds us, "Do good to all people, especially to those who belong to the family of believers." Be a difference-maker. Share encouragement and positivity within your sphere of influence.

What is meant for you
Will come in search of you...
But, unless the doors are open
It can never reach you..

Courage is Master Over Fear

Throughout my career, I've coached games, taught students, trained staff, delivered speeches, and called plays in front of tens of thousands of fans. Every situation came with nerves and anticipation. But I leaned on preparation, prayed for strength, and stayed focused. Courage doesn't mean you're never afraid, it means you trust your training enough to push through fear and reach your goals.

Courage is resistance to fear and mastery of fear—not absence of fear.

-Mark Twain

The Power of Positive Thinking

I'll never ask more from you than I ask from myself. In fact, I don't "ask" at all. I set goals and expect everyone to get on board. We're in this together. Positive thinking, paired with focused effort, can lead to extraordinary outcomes. Believe in it, because anything is possible.

I am realistic.
I expect miracles.

-Wayne Dyer.

Stay True to the Plan

Preparation is everything. If you think you're talented enough to "wing it," you're likely setting yourself up for failure. Great preparation often allows you to exceed expectations. So work hard, anticipate challenges, and stay driven.

An idiot with a plan can beat a genius without a plan.

-Warren Buffet

Guard Against Complacency

Never take your competition or adversaries lightly. Even those who seem the least threatening can catch you off guard if you're not careful. Stay alert, stay hungry, and prepare for their best shot, because complacency is the quickest path to failure.

-

And if you think tough men are dangerous, wait until you see what weak men are capable of.

Jordan Peterson

Praise, Reaffirmation, and Encouragement

We all come from different backgrounds, which means we all start from different places. That's why, as a leader, you must stay focused on the finish line. Changing an organization's culture starts with instilling personal responsibility and a strong work ethic. Encourage those you lead to pursue their goals with purpose. Your consistent praise, direction, and support can guide them toward lasting success, long after their time with you ends.

Our background and circumstances may have influenced who we are, but we are responsible for who we become.

-Barbara Geraci

It's NOT Your Place

As a teacher, I taught Government, Economics, U.S. History, World Geography, and Texas History. As a high school coach, I led teams in football, basketball, track, baseball, and golf. I also served as an Athletic Director, Safety Director, and Assistant Principal. Needless to say, my leadership experience in education was broad and varied.

Politically, I've always considered myself a moderate, bouncing between a conservative Democrat and a liberal Republican. I don't identify as an independent because our political system doesn't leave much room for them. But regardless of my personal beliefs, I always remained politically neutral in the classroom and on the field. These are places where we shape the minds of the next generation. As educators, it is not our role to influence political beliefs. That responsibility belongs to the parents or guardians.

The world is changed by your example not by your opinion.

-Paul Coelho

Direct Communication Is Best

I believe in being honest, direct, and assertive. That way, everyone knows where we stand. Respect is the starting point for any meaningful communication, and with me, you get it from the beginning. If it's not returned, I'll quickly adjust. I've been called difficult at times, and I accept that. But rarely does it begin from a place of disrespect.

The funny thing is, when you don't let people disrespect you, they start calling you difficult.

-Tom Hardy

Build a Bond with Them

When you're working with kids, remember that every one of them comes from a different background. To build trust and effective relationships, you have to listen, observe, and center your actions around their needs. You don't have to be their friend, but you *do* have to be a mentor they can count on.

People don't always need advice. Sometimes all they really need is a hand to hold, an ear to listen, and a hear to understand them.

Intent and Effort Are Deliberate

This was my guiding principle during my years as an educator: be your best every day. Intent and effort don't happen by accident, they're choices. And if you want to reach your goals, you have to pursue them consistently and deliberately.

Never compete with anyone, never try to be better than anyone, simply try to be better than the person you were yesterday.

Calculated Communication

This is a lesson I had to learn the hard way, more than once. As a leader, your words carry weight. Say what you mean, and mean what you say. Your tone and timing impact how others react. Often, the way one person responds affects the entire group. Know when to keep conversations private rather than making them public.

Be careful with your words. Once they are said, they can only be forgiven, not forgotten.

Individual Achievement Is Limitless

I've always believed that every student or athlete I've worked with has the potential to achieve something great. That's where I start when I mentor them. Many have gone on to live successful lives and careers. When they leave my guidance, I want them to believe that anything is possible, and that any goal is within reach.

A leader sees greatness in other people. He nor she can be much of a leader if all she sees is herself.

-Maya Angelou

Be Inquisitive About New Job Opportunities

When I consider a new opportunity, I pay close attention to the desire and commitment of the people I'm talking to. During interviews, I listen carefully to measure the sincerity of the administrators and committee. Do they truly want improvement? Are they committed to progress? A great leader needs a great team to lean on.

Hope is a hand that reaches between what is and what can be. It gently leads us onward when the path becomes hard to see.

-John Mark Green

Keep Them Focused on Progress

Every coach worries about complacency. A few wins, and players can start feeling too confident. A few losses, and they might stop caring. That's why the focus must always be *progress*. Win or lose, it's up to the head coach to evaluate, adjust, and emphasize effort and improvement. I've coached winless teams and championship teams. In the end, it's how you finish which counts.

Daily Reviews and Reflections Are Necessary

These moments are best done in solitude. As a leader, you must stay attuned to the needs and morale of your team, whether it's your staff, students, or athletes. They want to know you've got their back and can handle pressure. But they don't need access to your private doubts or emotions. When you model strength and empowerment, it gives others permission to feel empowered too.

Success is not permanent, and failure is not final. Never stop working after success, and never stop trying after failure.

Accentuate the Learning Experience

This is why I loved teaching and coaching. For students and athletes, success is built on a series of learning experiences. I always emphasized the value of learning from mistakes. If a player kept repeating the same error, I had to ask myself: Is my teaching effective? Sometimes the flaw is in the delivery; sometimes the student just isn't motivated. But either way, the key is to keep pushing toward progress.

I've failed over and over and over again in my life, and that's why I succeed.

No Risk It, No Biscuit!

When I first started coaching football at the young age of 20, I already knew what I wanted, I wanted to be a leader of young men and the head coach of my own team. Every step I took, every class I attended, and every job I accepted in those early years was part of a plan to make that dream a reality.

My first public school job had me wearing many hats. I coached junior high football, taught five classes, and then crossed the street to coach JV and Varsity linebackers. My days were often 14 hours long. On Thursday and Friday nights, I led the scout team while the Varsity played their games. Saturdays and Sundays were reserved for film breakdown, practice organization, and game planning for the next opponent, another 10 hours each day.

I was learning my craft well.

Still, when I told fellow coaches my goal was to lead my own program within five years, they laughed. Some even scoffed. But at 26, it was announced in the local paper that I had been hired as the new Athletic Director and Head Football Coach at a city school. Nobody was laughing then.

In fact, my phone wouldn't stop ringing. Many of those same people now wanted to join me. I listened, evaluated each person's commitment, and selected only a few to bring on board. The ones who scoffed never really had a shot.

Together, we turned that program around and won a lot of games.

There's a saying: *"No risk it, no biscuit."* If you believe in yourself: be bold, stay positive, and put yourself out there.

Sometimes, life is about risking everything for a dream no one can see but you.

Political Destruction – A Test of Commitment

I hope you never have to experience a situation like this, professionally or personally. It was one of the hardest moments of my career.

As the Athletic Director of a major 5A athletic program, I was called into a meeting with my superintendent. There, he informed me that the school board had decided to defund and disband all extracurricular activities for the upcoming year. Fall practices were just days away.

He handed me a list of directives (which I recorded and documented in disbelief). The two most significant: send all staff home, despite already starting work, and cancel every game, tournament, and contract across all programs. I walked out of his office, called an emergency staff meeting, explained the situation, and sent everyone home.

But I didn't carry out the rest of the directives. I didn't agree with them.

Instead, I found another job, prepared my family to move, and showed up the next morning to submit my resignation. That's when the superintendent told me I needed to attend an emergency school board meeting. He escorted me to the room.

Every board member, central office staff, and TEA (Texas Education Agency) monitor was already seated. When we arrived, I handed my resignation to the superintendent. But he told me to sit at the far end of the table.

The meeting began with accusations that I had spoken to the press and misrepresented the situation. The truth? A reporter called me the night before, claiming the superintendent and board president had blamed me directly for sending staff home and canceling contracts. I told him that wasn't true, and that I had proof. I played the recording.

He promised to report only what the tape showed. And the next morning, it was all over the front page of San Antonio's major newspaper. That article triggered the emergency meeting.

At first, the board and TEA monitors didn't believe me. But I had come prepared.

I played the recording for everyone in the room.

The silence afterward was deafening. Some administrators and board members cried. The TEA monitors took control of the meeting from that point on.

Despite everything, I helped them rebuild the budget, salaries, and contracts for all extracurricular programs. It became more of a negotiation, with the TEA mediating. We ended up with about 65% of the previous year's funding.

It was a nightmare, but I did what needed to be done.

At the end of the meeting, I stood up, reiterated my resignation, and walked out.

While I was packing my office, one of the TEA monitors knocked on the door. He asked me to sit with him. Then he pulled out his phone, dialed a number, and put it on speaker.

It was Dr. Mike Mosley, the TEA Commissioner.

After a brief introduction, he got straight to the point: he asked me to stay. He said the programs had no chance without my help. When I told him I had accepted another position and already resigned, he said, "About that...I called the superintendent of the district that offered you the job and told them you're not taking it."

He told me my current contract was binding, that I wasn't going anywhere, and that from now on, I'd have direct access to his office. No more interference from the board. Then he hung up.

I had no choice but to stay.

We started over from scratch, with the students, with the community. In the first three years, our football record was 0–10, then 3–7, then 5–5. This was after being District Champions just before the whole ordeal. But in the three years that followed, we raised five more championship banners in the gym.

I moved on soon after. But that chapter taught me more about commitment, leadership, and politics than any textbook ever could.

People left when the house was falling apart, not knowing
I was tearing it down to build a mansion, I just wanted to
see who was gonna grab a hammer.

Giving Up Is NEVER an Option

I was once the head football coach of a team that gave up an average of 58 points per game during the district schedule. After the season ended, I met with our building and trades teacher and asked if he could help us create a visual reminder of that painful season. He agreed to build six wooden signs: each one representing a team that had beaten us. He burned in the opponents' names and final scores, then varnished and finished the boards beautifully. He brought them to the weight room over Christmas break, and together, we hung them from the ceiling to the wall right by the entrance.

When the players returned, I gathered them in the weight room. We all stared at those signs, and right then, we agreed on a motto. Every time a player left a workout; they would slap the signs and shout: **"NEVER AGAIN!"**

By the end of the next season, we had beaten five of the six teams on those boards. The only one we lost was a close 25-21 game, a game we nearly won.

Giving up is NEVER an option. If you get knocked down, dust yourself off and get back in the fight. I've never had any tolerance for quitters.

Know Your Triggers

We all have triggers, and they can interfere with how we work with kids. As a mentor and educator, you must **know your own triggers** before stepping into any classroom, field, or court. Some students will try to find those weak spots from day one. That's just the reality.

During our first staff meetings each year, we ran role-playing exercises simulating those first critical days of school. I'd use my most experienced staff members to play the students, helping new or struggling teachers navigate difficult scenarios. Then we'd give constructive feedback and help them develop calm, controlled responses.

Was it a popular training? Not at all. But weeks later, some of those same teachers would come back and say, "Thank you."

My advice: never let them see you sweat.

We're not ourselves when we're triggered -
We become who we think
We need to SURVIVE.
And when we're constantly being triggered,
Our identity can start to slip away—
Because our personality and values are constantly getting hijacked by fight-or-flight reflexes.

-Dr. Glenn Patrick Doyle.

Be the Example – Influence Them

As an educational leader, you are a role model, whether you like it or not. Your influence stretches across your community, administration, staff, students, and athletes. That responsibility comes with the role.

I can't count how many times a young adult has walked up and said, "Do you remember me?" Most of the time, I didn't, having taught and coached thousands over 40 years. But I'd always ask for their name or a memory. They'd usually share a positive moment, and once reminded, I often recalled the situation. We'd have a great conversation before going our separate ways.

It's a humbling reminder: **you never know who you're influencing.** So, stay positive and always demand excellence.

Professional Ambition and Goals

To all young professionals reading this: **Be bold. Be confident.**

Don't be afraid to move up the ladder or seek the right job opportunity. Develop your skills, work hard, and make sound decisions when chances come your way. I'm not talking about trying to suck up your way to the top. I'm talking about earning respect through consistent, dependable contributions.

Let your actions speak for you. If they're overlooked where you are, don't worry, another opportunity will come along. One that fits your expertise and values. Just be ready to take it.

What you do speaks so loudly that I cannot hear what you say.

-Ralph Waldo Emerson

I Don't Believe in Luck

I don't believe in luck or blind optimism.

What I *do* believe in is **hard work and determination**, especially when they meet opportunity. That's when success follows. I believe in divine intervention, too, I know God has a plan for each of us. But He never promised a rose garden.

You've got to listen with your soul, and be willing to obey.

A man cannot directly choose his circumstances, but he can choose his thoughts, and so indirectly, yet surely, shape his circumstances.

-James Allen

Handling Losses and Disappointments

Let's talk about that look on a coach's face after a tough loss, whether close or a blowout. There's no hiding it. That disappointment is real. But how you **respond** in that team meeting afterward makes all the difference.

You have two choices:

Option 1: Lose your temper. Lash out. Berate the players. Point fingers.

This is what inexperienced coaches often do, and it almost never works. Players tune you out. You lose them.

Option 2: Take a breath. Compose yourself. Then gather the team and remind them:

"We win together. We lose together."

Offer a brief, honest assessment of areas that need improvement. Promise that you and the staff will review the film and prepare a plan to get better. Most importantly, let them know how much you care about them, and that you're committed to helping them improve.

If you have individual concerns, address those privately. Have one-on-one or small group meetings if needed.

It's okay to show disappointment, but don't forget to **build hope**. You create a winning culture by emphasizing growth, effort, and unity.

Strength in Dark Times

I love this quote from *Alice in Wonderland*! My close family and friends understand the depth of my relationship with them. I carry each of them in my heart, and I'll stand by them through sickness, hard times, and even death. My memories of them will remain kind and enduring long after they're gone.

Yes, there have been moments in my life when my heart and health couldn't bear the weight of grief. Still, there have also been losses where I stayed present right up to the end. Life isn't always about the good times. Sometimes, spiritual love means showing up in the darkest of times.

As **II Corinthians 1:4–8** reminds us, God is always with us. He strengthens our spirit, especially when we feel weakest.

When you can't look on the bright side,
I will sit with you in the dark.

Dealing With Tragic Loss

This brings to mind several tragedies I witnessed while serving as an athletic director. These moments are etched into my heart.

One devastating day, a young sophomore basketball player collapsed and died during a home game. We later learned he had an aortic aneurysm, a hidden heart defect. He passed away in front of his teammates and coaches. The shock, grief, and fallout within our community were immediate and deeply felt.

The year before, tragedy struck again. The booster club president, also a close friend and the parent of one of our football players, was killed in front of the school. It was game day, around 3 p.m. He was trying to cross the freeway and was struck by another vehicle. He died instantly.

Later in my career, another moment tested us. Our team was coming off the field at halftime when I was flagged down. I was told that one of our star player's mothers had been killed in a car accident on her way to the game. His father was already waiting at the gate to take him home. They were both incredibly supportive parents, and I wanted to be there when the news was delivered.

We brought the player to a quiet spot behind the fieldhouse. I asked the coaches to take the rest of the team inside. His father arrived, and with all the strength he could muster, told his son that his mother hadn't made it. I'll never forget their reactions, the raw emotion, the embrace, and the tears we all shared.

Afterward, father and son made a powerful decision: she would've wanted him to finish the game in her honor. I was hesitant, but after praying with them, I listened to that inner voice telling me to follow their lead.

With little time left, I gathered the team in the locker room and explained the situation. There wasn't a dry eye. We invited the father and son in, and together we said the Lord's Prayer. It was the loudest and most heartfelt prayer I've ever experienced. Then the team rallied behind him, we scored 35 unanswered points in the second half and came back to beat a tough opponent.

After everyone left, our coaching staff stood together in a circle. We held hands, and I offered a prayer for strength and clarity for what we had just experienced.

I didn't respond the same way to the first two tragedies. I wasn't always sure how to handle the heartbreak. But I've since learned, there are no perfect answers. Only God knows the time appointed for each of us. What we can do while we're still here is offer spiritual love and be a comforter to those in need.

Our Father, Who art in heaven, hallowed be Thy name; Thy kingdom come; Thy will be done on earth as it is in heaven. Give us this day our daily bread; and forgive us our trespasses as we forgive those who trespass against us; and lead us not into temptation, but deliver us from evil.

Amen

A Caring Disposition

Throughout my career in education and leadership, I've had countless conversations with staff and students during times of need. I've come to believe that empathy and genuine friendship are essential in building strong relationships.

In fact, I'm convinced that God sends us angels in our lowest moments—when our spiritual light begins to fade. **Luke 22:43** tells us that even Jesus was strengthened by an angel in his time of trial.

You can't be an effective leader without a caring heart. For some, this comes naturally. For others, it takes effort—especially if they were raised in environments that didn't nurture emotional expression. Either way, it's a vital skill to develop and rely on.

"Today was a Difficult Day," said Pooh.

There was a pause.

"Do you want to talk about it?" asked Piglet.

"No," said Pooh after a bit. "No, I don't think I do."

"That's okay," said Piglet, and he came and sat beside his friend.

"What are you doing?" asked Pooh.

"Nothing, really," said Piglet. "Only, I know what Difficult Days are like. I quite often don't feel like talking about them either.

"But goodness," continued Piglet, "Difficult Days are so much easier when you know you've got someone there for you. And I'll always be here for you, Pooh."

And as Pooh sat there, working through his Difficult Day while Piglet quietly swung his little legs beside him... he realized his friend had never been more right.

Mental Toughness Starts With Belief

I read this poem in college over 40 years ago, and it's stuck with me ever since. It became my personal mantra, something I passed on to every coach, player, and student I worked with.

I once took a football team of 15 players into a game against a powerhouse team with 65 players. At halftime, we were down 0–7, and I could see doubt written across their faces. That's when I gave the most passionate speech of my career.

I told them: *"There are only 11 players allowed on the field from each team. It doesn't matter how many they have on the bench; it only takes our 11 to beat their 65."*

In the second half, we shut them out and came back to win 14–7. That day, those 15 young men learned a lifelong lesson about belief, effort, and mental toughness, lessons they've carried with them for more than 30 years.

Thinking
by Walter D. Wintle

If you think you are beaten, you are;
If you think you dare not, you don't.
If you'd like to win, but think you can't,
It's almost a cinch you won't.

If you think you'll lose, you're lost,
For out of the world we find
Success begins with a fellow's will
-It's all in the state of mind.

If you think you're outclassed, you are;
You've got to think high to rise;
You've got to be sure of yourself before
You can ever win a prize.

Life's battles don't always go
To the stronger or faster man;
But soon or late the man who wins,
Is the one who thinks he can.

FAITHFUL GUIDANCE

Faith & Courage

Anyone who has worked with me, been coached by me, or learned under my guidance will tell you—I've always been fiercely competitive and deeply determined. I never led with flash or arrogance, but with quiet strength and purpose. I consistently modeled and instilled confidence, character, commitment, and genuine care. I never believed in giving in to adversity. Instead of fate, I chose faith. **Mark 9:23** has always guided me: *"Jesus said to him, 'If you can believe, all things are possible to him who believes.'"* My faith was, and still is, a cornerstone in every environment I've led, whether with staff or students.

All According to His Plan

I believe that God has a purpose for each of us. He gifted us with free will and a guiding conscience. If we truly tune into the Holy Spirit, and listen with an open heart, the path before us becomes clear. I encourage you to lean into your heart's calling. It holds the blueprint for your influence, your purpose, and your success.

Your Values Reflect Your Soul

I grew up in a home that faced economic hardship but was rich in foundational values. From a young age, I was taught the essentials: respect, discipline, and commitment. Alongside these values, I also came to understand the complexities of emotional struggle: Irish temperament, alcoholism, and abuse. These experiences gave me clarity about the kind of person I wanted to become, and the kind I didn't.

On the field, I was different. There, I could channel my anger and intensity in a productive way. It was my release. But as I grew into a head coaching role, I began to understand how to balance intensity with intentionality. I used my own story to help young men define their boundaries, their values, and their identities.

Plant the Seeds of Expectation and Growth

Throughout my career, I've had the privilege of working with outstanding educators and mentors who shaped my philosophy. I've strived to be a motivator, a patient encourager, a listening ear, and, when needed, a firm father figure. Whether working with staff, students, or athletes, I planted seeds of high expectations and nurtured the potential within each individual.

Now, many years later, I look at the lives that have flourished from those seeds, and I am humbled. If you were ever part of that growth, please know that I am forever grateful for the opportunity to walk beside you. You are part of my daily prayers.

Walk with Faith and Strength

As a man of faith, I'm constantly aware of the challenges and negative forces that exist in our world. But every morning, I rise with purpose. My confidence, my strength, and my spirit are rooted in something greater than myself. As it says in **Matthew 28:20:** *"And surely I am with you always, to the very end of the age."*

Be Grounded in Purpose

Over the decades, I've experienced the full spectrum of life, its highs and its hardships. Like anyone, I've faced discouragement, disappointment, and doubt. But I've leaned heavily on my friends, my colleagues, and above all, my faith. In **Colossians 3:23–24,** we are reminded: *"Whatever you do, work at it with all your heart, as working for the Lord, not for human masters."* This verse reminded me daily to stay focused on the higher calling.

As a young professional, I didn't chase approval. Instead, I asked questions, worked hard, volunteered, and learned. I stayed hungry to grow, yet grounded in humility. That mindset has never left me. To young educators and coaches: stay curious, stay faithful, and never stop learning.

Faith and Belief

If there's one lesson, I hope every young coach hears, it's this: your players need to know you believe in them. Each one brings their strengths and struggles, but all of them are looking for someone to see their potential.

I'll never forget one game, late in the season. We had a narrow lead with just over a minute left and faced a 4th down deep in our own territory. I was preparing to send out the punt team, when my running back pushed through the huddle and said, *"Coach, believe in me. Give me the ball, we'll get the first down and win this game."*

I saw the fire in his eyes, and I realized, this moment meant everything. I changed the play, put the game in his hands. He took the handoff, broke a tackle, and sprinted 86 yards for the touchdown. After scoring, he ran along the sideline, found me, and threw his arms around me: *"Do you believe in me now, Coach? I'll never let you down."*

That season, he became the first 2,000-yard rusher in school history, and we made a deep playoff run. But more importantly, we built something powerful: trust, belief, and lifelong impact.

Spiritual Calm

In life's darkest hours, when the weight of the world seems unbearable, I find refuge in my faith and inner strength. Even when the storm rages around me, there is a quiet, unshakable calm that anchors my soul. God has a way of covering us, even when everything else seems to be falling apart. I've faced these moments, both personally and professionally, where the pressure was intense, and chaos surrounded me. People often ask, "How do you stay calm and composed when everything's on the line?" The truth is simple: I pause, breathe deeply, whisper a prayer for guidance, and walk forward: not alone, but as a warrior led by faith.

Inner Voice, Spiritual Connections

This world is smaller than it appears, especially when seen through the eyes of faith. The paths we walk and the people we meet are not random. I believe the Lord weaves divine appointments into our daily lives, spiritual connections meant to inspire, guide, or even test us. But these connections require a quiet heart and a listening spirit. If you slow down long enough to hear your inner voice, you'll find that God is speaking, and when He does, don't ignore the moment. Recognize it, embrace it, and let it shape you.

Let Faith Silence the Doubt

We are all human. We stumble, we second-guess, and we carry the weight of insecurity as we learn and grow. But faith has the power to lift us beyond self-doubt. Through experiences, mentors, and mistakes, we build the foundation of who we are meant to be. I've learned that faith isn't the absence of fear. It's the courage to move forward despite it. Let your belief in something greater than yourself shape your confidence, character, and calling.

Impressions and Standards

Looking back on a long journey through education and leadership, I often reflect on the purpose God had for me. I truly believe He used me, not for my perfection, but for my willingness to serve, to uplift, and to offer hope. I wasn't always the most emotionally expressive person, but I led with sincerity and a deep commitment to reflect His light. For young coaches and teachers: you have the power to leave lasting impressions. Set high standards. Be a model of consistency, kindness, and integrity. Some of the most beautiful memories I carry are of those whose spirits shined with goodness. I can only hope my influence brought the same light into your life.

Empathy and Spiritual Strength Are Essential

Coaches are often seen through the lens of wins and losses, but the true test of a leader comes when life hits hard. Over the years, I've had to navigate more than just games, I've stood by young people in times of death, divorce, tragedy, and trauma. Moments that break hearts and shake foundations. These are not in the job description, but they are part of the calling. It's in these moments that empathy and spiritual strength are not just needed, they are essential. As a leader, I had to stretch the limits of my heart, make room to console, to guide, to simply be present. Because how you respond in adversity will forever define the trust others place in you.

Guiding Principle

My guiding principle, especially in the later chapters of my life, has been rooted in faith. I've endured pain, setbacks, and personal challenges, some genetic, others the result of choices I made. But always, God gave me the strength to rise again. One verse in particular carried me through the toughest moments:

Hebrews 11:1 – "Now faith is the assurance of things hoped for, the conviction of things not seen."

Faith reminded me that hope was not gone, just unseen. That even in failure, I could start again. Trusting in God's timing, I found the courage to keep going.

Your Selflessness Matters

When you're young and driven, pouring everything into your work, your team, and your purpose, you may feel invisible at times. The world doesn't always applaud effort, and some people may never understand your heart. But remember, **God does.** He sees every late night, every sacrifice, every moment you show up even when it's hard. Your dedication matters. Even when it isn't acknowledged, it's making a difference. Stay the course, trust your spirit, and keep showing up. You are planting seeds that will grow in ways you may never fully see, but rest assured, they matter.

Genuinely Forgive, Never Forget

Throughout my career, I've always tried to lead with integrity and respect. But good intentions are not always seen through the same lens, especially by those with conflicting motives. At some point in your journey, you'll be faced with difficult decisions that prioritize the well-being of the group over the comfort of individuals. Those decisions can invite opposition, and sometimes, powerful resistance. I've been there. I've felt the sting of betrayal, the frustration of being undermined. I carried that anger at first. It burned quietly, eating away at my peace. But over time, I learned that true healing only comes through genuine forgiveness. Not for their sake, but for mine. Letting go of the weight doesn't mean forgetting. I've never forgotten, and I don't intend to. To forget would be to forfeit the lesson. Every trial grew me. Every scar strengthened my resolve. When one door closed, God opened another, where my leadership, knowledge, and spirit were needed. And so, I kept moving forward.

Reflections and Memories

My body may have slowed down, but my mind remains full and sharp. I carry with me an entire lifetime of memories, bright, beautiful, and sacred. Thousands of students, hundreds of colleagues, countless moments that shaped not only their lives but also mine. When I look back, my heart is filled with gratitude. I see God's grace in every turn, every intersection, every name and face I was lucky enough to know. Scripture tells us in **2 Corinthians 9:8** that God will bless us abundantly, in all things, at all times, and I've lived that truth. I was given so much more than I ever asked for. Friendships that strengthened me, opportunities that humbled me, and a calling that filled my life with purpose. To all who were part of that journey, you were no accident. You were divinely placed. And I thank you, from the depths of my heart.

Concern and Passion

I may not have been the most outwardly emotional leader, but make no mistake, my concern ran deep. Many of you witnessed it, not in hugs or tears, but in the quiet consistency of how I showed up for you. Day after day. Concern, by its true definition, is a state of care, born out of connection, affection, and responsibility. It's one of the foundational pillars of any transformative culture. Over four decades, I tried to instill that concern in others by modeling it myself. Through example and encouragement, I passed on what I knew: courage, loyalty, and love.

As **1 Corinthians 13** so beautifully reminds us:

"Love is patient, love is kind... it is not easily angered, it keeps no record of wrongs."

That scripture reflects the kind of love I aspired to give. Imperfect? Yes. But sincere. My efforts may have fallen short at times, but they always came from a place of genuine care.

I am not my scars, although they are poured into the foundation of my being.
I am not my pain, though it leads me through the dark shadows my light gets to follow.
I am not my fears, for they fester in the eye of my ego.

I am my courageous heart, learning to lead with love.

-M.G. Williams

A Simple Gesture Goes a Long Way

Leadership isn't just about strategy or structure, it's about sensitivity. Every person you encounter is fighting a battle you may not see. Life has a way of challenging us in private. As a leader, it's your responsibility to remain attuned to the quiet cues: the slumped shoulders, the silences, the subtle cries for grace. A kind word, a hand on a shoulder, a moment of understanding, these small gestures can leave an unforgettable mark. You don't need to accept every excuse, but you can offer empathy. Compassion doesn't weaken discipline; it deepens trust.

Nobody has it easy. Everyone has issues. Life happens. You never know what people are going through, so pause before you start judging, mocking, or criticizing others. Everybody is fighting their own war.

Concern – The Team-First Concept

There's something wrong with your character if opportunity controls your loyalty.

Teaching selflessness is no easy task, especially in an achievement-driven world. Every player wants to be seen. Every individual wants their efforts acknowledged. But as a coach, I knew this truth: true success only happens when personal pride is set aside for the greater good. A team that plays as one will always outperform a group of stars chasing their own glory. And those who truly serve the team? Their recognition always comes. The game sees it. The coaches see it. And most importantly, the team feels it. Wins are sweeter when they're shared. Losses, easier to bear. Because in the end, it's never about me. It's always about *we*.

Initiate Camaraderie

Brace yourself team building is coming

As a coach, an administrator, and a leader, I learned that camaraderie isn't something that just happens, it has to be intentionally cultivated. A thriving program is built on shared goals, mutual respect, and loyalty. Without that foundation, long-term success is impossible. It falls on the leader to spark that connection, to nurture it, to model it in every interaction. Whether in the locker room, on the field, or in the staff meeting, unity begins at the top. And when people feel seen, heard, and valued, they show up not just for the job, but for each other.

THE FOUR PILLARS OF SUCCESS

The Four Pillars of Success: Cultural Reality

My career as an educator took an early turn when I realized the impact my efforts had on those within my sphere of influence. As I studied the intricacies of various cultures, I came to understand that, despite the differences, many shared some common threads. When I speak of culture, I'm referring to the full spectrum of ways of life: arts, beliefs, and institutions, passed down from generation to generation.

Many students and athletes come from home environments lacking basic socioeconomic stability and moral structure. We cannot assume that young people grow up with the same behaviors, values, and expectations that shaped us. After careful observation and research, my inner circle and I developed four foundational pillars to effect positive cultural change within our programs: **confidence, character, commitment, and concern**. I will be discussing these pillars in greater detail in my future observations. When combined with eternal optimism and a strong vision, these qualities create a powerful pathway to success.

The Four Pillars: Confidence, Character, Commitment, Concern

This message is for anyone who has faced challenges and obstacles in life. We each walk a unique path, one often marked by struggles related to spiritual health, family, and professional responsibilities. At times, the weight of it all can feel overwhelming. In those moments, I've leaned on my faith for strength and direction. **Isaiah 41:10** reminds us that God is always with us; He will strengthen and help us in difficult times.

Success, to me, means making meaningful progress and influencing others for the better. Of course, personal excellence and winning matter, but they are not everything. My priority has always been to help others develop **confidence, character, commitment, and concern**. These are the core values that build lasting success.

To those I've mentored over the years: I trust many of you have built incredible lives. My only request is that you **pay it forward**, use your influence to uplift others, just as others once did for you.

A Lifetime of Skills

I first learned this lesson as a high school athlete. There were coaches I would've run through a brick wall for, and a few whose impact left lasting negative impressions. When I committed to becoming a coach during college, I remembered the worst coach I had, and I vowed to be the exact opposite.

I chose to be a **relationship builder**, someone who uplifted young people with encouragement and high expectations. I set out to instill qualities like **confidence, commitment, character, and concern**, aiming to develop well-rounded individuals. For more than four decades, I've walked this path with countless young men and women. We built them up, disciplined them, encouraged them, and pushed them toward their goals with love and conviction.

Coaching has been one of the most **rewarding and fulfilling experiences** of my life.

Willing Spirits of Success

This message is for all the teachers, coaches, and players I've had the honor of working with over the past 40 years. I did my best to give each of you opportunities for **growth**, **development**, and **success**.

It was always my intention to emphasize the importance of the four pillars: **confidence, character, commitment, and concern**. I hoped these values would help you become productive, compassionate adults in a free society.

Though our paths may have diverged, please know I've not forgotten any of you. Each of you holds a special place in my heart. This is my way of saying, from the bottom of my heart, **thank you.**

Confidence: The First Step to Success

When I accepted a new job in a new community, I knew that my first challenge would be to evaluate and build the **confidence** of everyone involved: staff, players, students, administrators, and the broader community.

From the very beginning, I implemented strategies to boost self-belief. It always started with preparation, supported by positive thinking and encouragement. Then came the need for a stronger work ethic. Next, we established attainable goals, starting small, then growing into larger shared achievements.

Every individual's preparation and effort contributed to the collective goal. When opportunity arose, success was not a matter of "luck", it was the result of preparation and the **confidence** that had been built.

Be Confident

Confidence and more specifically, **self-confidence**, is a cornerstone of building a successful program. As a leader, you must consistently demonstrate a confident, positive attitude. Your example sets the tone for everyone else. This isn't about arrogance. It's about being visible, encouraging, and **steadfast in your belief** in the team and its mission.

Confidence is a Superpower

Confidence is a crucial ingredient in transforming a community's culture. As an educator, I often took on roles in programs that required redirection and renewal. One of my first tasks was always to instill a **positive mindset** in everyone involved.

As a change agent, you must rely on **positive reinforcement, encouragement, and praise**. Change is never easy, but by coaxing others forward, step by step, you help them build the self-confidence they need to grow, succeed, and lead.

Building Confidence

To all young teachers and coaches: words and attitudes can be the enemy of sportsmanship and success. Build confidence and character in your kids. Keep them humble and hungry while focusing on progress and team goals. In today's world, there is too much vocal and physical banter between fans, players, and coaches. As an athletic director and head coach, my emphasis was always: *"Do your best, and don't sweat the rest."* Performance always trumps finger-pointing and attitude.

If your athletes want to celebrate, let them do it with their teammates. There was no place in our program for arrogance, taunting, or disrespect toward opponents. However, our opponents knew they were in for a hard and tough competition every time they came to play us. Our goal was to make them *dread* having to face us on our turf. Our confidence and determination spoke louder than any words ever could.

Instilling Confidence

Confidence means feeling sure of yourself and your abilities. It is a cornerstone of success for any program I've built. It's the first of the four components I believe are necessary to initiate a culture change. The others are character, commitment, and concern. But I always start by building confidence in staff, participants, and parents.

This includes techniques such as positive reinforcement, self-awareness, goal setting (starting with small steps), team-building exercises, physical and mental strength training, improved listening skills, speed and agility drills, and encouraging self-discipline. These must be consistently drilled and practiced. The more they become part of a daily routine and expectation, the more confident everyone becomes.

Failure Isn't an Option

When you're teaching or coaching kids who haven't experienced much success, you must build their confidence. As a coach or teacher, you should emphasize an *us-against-the-world* mindset every single day. In every strength and conditioning workout, every practice, and every pregame warm-up, you must be positive but firm.

An aura of determination and belief must underpin the team's will to win. That surrounding energy will spread throughout the team and become a powerful motivator.

Confidence Is Contagious

I was the Athletic Director and Head Football Coach at a large San Antonio school district. As the administrator and supervisor at high school basketball games, I was usually responsible for crowd control after the final buzzer. I would often stay behind to visit with players and walk them to the parking lot before securing the building.

One evening, as I walked with several players to a van waiting to take them home, the mother behind the wheel leaned out the window and said, *"Coach, I hope you know how much influence you have on our boys. As y'all walked to the van, I noticed they all have your same confident, distinct walk!"*

I chuckled and thanked her. But it reminded me of something important: you must always be aware of the impression you leave on kids. So, keep it positive and focused.

Confidence – Sustaining the Momentum

Most head coaches know that setting standards and expectations is only the beginning. The real work comes in building and maintaining a team throughout the season. This requires instilling confidence and cultivating trust among teammates so they can rely on each other and overcome adversity. When that trust and confidence are in place, anything, including great victories, is possible.

Character

Character is how someone thinks, feels, and behaves. I describe it as knowing the difference between right and wrong, and then choosing to do what's right, more often than not. It means accepting that mistakes will happen, but not allowing excuses to become the norm.

It also means facing consequences with the understanding that your behavior must improve. Character is one of the four pillars I emphasize when working to change the culture of a program.

Character – Display Your Intentions

My first job as an athletic director and head football coach was a true building project. To generate support for our first home game, I gathered all the coaches and players and loaded them onto four school buses in the heat of August. We drove to each of the four towns that made up the district and walked block by block, going door to door.

Each player delivered a calendar featuring our team photo and schedule, along with a personal invitation to attend the game. It took over four hours to complete.

When I arrived, the school had a long history of losses. Morale, discipline, and confidence were low. My first priority was to introduce the four pillars: confidence, commitment, character, and concern. We hired a competent and dedicated coaching staff that became my inner circle.

Then we went to work building an unmatched work ethic and an environment of respect, encouragement, and sportsmanship. Within a few years, the transformation was clear. Our programs produced 19 district, area, bi-district, and regional championships across multiple boys' and girls' sports.

Even more rewarding: 25 years later, the children of those former players won championships of their own in various sports. Champions, it turns out, pass on expectations and values to help their children become champions. That's what I call *changing a culture*. It's real, and it can happen in your community too.

Your Character Is Who You Are

I've served as a leader in several different environments and with many staffs. I never put much stock in a perceived reputation. If you are doing the right things with good intent, then your integrity allows your character to shine. I believe a person of good character can establish a reputation that is admired and modeled.

The strongest people are not those who show strength in front of us, but those who win battles we know nothing about.

Let Your Character Guide You

This lesson is for all the young coaches and teachers who are following my message. You should approach your job with your own character as your guide. I like to describe character as your intent to do the right thing, regardless of the opinions and actions of others. If you are asserting your character in the decision-making process, some will like you and some will not.

There are many participants and parents who support your rules and expectations, until you have to apply them to *their* situation. Then, you often fall out of favor. Some will sulk and stomp around, while others will take your actions as a learning experience.

I like to say that you only have five years to implement and initiate a cultural change in a program. After that, you will likely have accumulated as many enemies as you have allies. So be aware: your time as a leader of change will eventually come to an end.

One week, they love me.

Next week, they hate me.

Both weeks, I get paid.

Focus on Doing the Right Thing

Lol! This illustration is pretty close to reality. There were times in my career as a leader when negative information filtered back to me. I learned early on that it was a waste of time to be confrontational about disloyalty.

So, I would occasionally slip some information out through a meeting or one-on-one conversation. It was always interesting to see how that information would circulate and eventually return to me. Many times, it was just good to know who you could count on and who you could not.

I adopted the old philosophy: *"Keep your friends close, and your enemies even closer."* This information was useful in the strategic game of leadership. But most of the time, I simply focused on doing the right thing and let the rest take care of itself. It really does take too much time and energy to chase negativity.

Be an Independent Thinker

As an educator and father, I tried to emphasize the importance of being an independent thinker while staying true to yourself. Everyone has a choice: be yourself, or let someone influence you to become someone you're not.

A good leader respects others but stands out front with their own standards and ethics. You're either an influencer or a follower.

Focus on the Needs of Others

Part of changing a program's culture is to install a system of character, one that emphasizes a person's virtue over their disobedience and despair. It should establish the expectation of making a positive effort to do the right thing.

Create an environment of respect, concern, and commitment to one another. Encourage participants to focus on the needs of others instead of themselves.

If you are the leader, believe that you are the agent of change. Be an effective role model, and expect your staff to be the same.

Be a Product of Your Faith

When I was a young professional, I used to describe myself as fearless. I was never intimidated by nervousness or negative thoughts. I welcomed the opportunity to be the difference-maker. Like everyone, I got the jitters and performance anxiety, but I maintained my focus and moved forward. For those of you who find yourselves in similar situations, know that God will never forsake you — **Deuteronomy 31:6–8**. In the second half of my career, I realized that I was not a fearless individual. My strength and focus were actually products of my faith.

Learn to Lean on Your Faith

Our character and integrity are tested daily when you are an effective educator. Students, parents, and staff challenge your leadership and organizational skills every day. That's why preparation and anticipation are key elements of your success. Don't let your ego or temper get in your way. First, pause and take a deep breath. Then move forward with your plan, with intent and goodwill. Stay focused, redirect behaviors without hesitation, then continue moving forward. I try to say a quick prayer while searching for my inner voice. Be strong in your faith, because He will draw near to you for protection and purpose — James 4:8.

I said that prayer and gathered my strength when I received a phone call from our head boys' basketball coach. I was the athletic director, and it was my night off. Our teams were playing a triple-header in the arena. He called in despair and with a bit of panic to let me know that one of our players had collapsed on the sideline while inbounding a pass to his teammate. It happened right in front of him, and our athletic trainer responded immediately from the bench. The trainer radioed from the floor for an ambulance and started CPR. He told the coach to clear the floor and whispered that the player did not have a pulse. The coach cleared the floor and the arena by asking everyone to leave. Soon, the ambulance arrived, continued CPR, loaded him, and headed to the hospital.

I asked the head coach which hospital, and he told me. We agreed to meet there in 30 minutes. He had the assistant coaches empty the facility and lock up. A few months earlier, I had heart surgery, so physically I was still pretty weak. When I got to the hospital ER, I went through the routine I mentioned above. After a short prayer, I got out of the truck and walked toward the emergency room.

The head coach met me at the door to share what he knew before I went in. The EMT had told him the player was DOA and that they were unable to revive him. He told me the player's parents were inside the room with the doctors. He also said the ER waiting room was full of players and concerned parents, somewhere around 60 people. He gave me all this information with tears in his eyes and distress on his face. I asked him to gather himself and sit with the players and families while I went in to speak with the parents of the deceased player.

I did just that. They received me with gracious sorrow and disbelief. I grabbed them both by the hands and expressed my deep sorrow through tears of strength. Then I asked them to pray with me, they agreed. I spoke from my inner voice and asked Jesus to lovingly receive their son's soul while we asked for some understanding. After the prayer, I explained the concern of the community and let them know there were at least 60 people in the waiting room without answers. The father asked me to give them a few minutes, and then he would come out to meet everyone and announce his son's passing. Then he looked at me and requested that I lead them all in the Lord's Prayer. I agreed and went out to meet the crowd.

When I got out there, the questions and comments were overwhelming. I calmed everyone down and let them know the father would be out shortly to speak with us all. I was disturbed by the negative comments about the game officials and the rough play of our opponents. While waiting, I asked our head coach whether the game had been videotaped. He said it had, and that I could view it later that night. However, he didn't believe the negative comments were accurate or warranted.

Eventually, the father came out to address the crowd in the ER waiting room. He was gracious and thanked everyone for their concern. Unfortunately, he confirmed that their son had passed away. The room erupted into tears and sobbing. We were blessed to have a lot of parents there with us. After a few minutes, the father gathered everyone around. He asked everyone to participate in the Lord's Prayer, led by me. The room grew silent for a moment, then I began, "Our Father, who art in Heaven..."

The voices were loud and in unison. Goosebumps and chills came over me as we finished. There were lots of tears, hugs, and some audible sobs. Eventually, everyone went home.

The basketball coach and I went back to work. We returned to the arena and watched the videotape three or four times. I didn't see anything on tape that could have caused his death. Early the next morning, my phone rang off the hook: the superintendent, principal, board members, officials' association, and newspaper were all calling, wanting answers. I explained my actions and findings, and told them it must have been something unrelated to officiating or game play.

I was under a lot of pressure to provide answers I didn't have. A few weeks later, we received the results of the autopsy report. It turned out that the player had an aortic aneurysm he was born with, and it ruptured inside his heart. He died instantly, and it just happened to be while playing the sport he loved.

I wanted to tell this story because it was such an unusual and difficult situation to navigate. The Lord knows my feet were clearly in the fire, and I fully relied on my inner spirit to guide me through. I believe that all His believers have this ability, and God needs you to know that it's part of His plan.

Character Starts With Integrity

I like this quote because it reflects my philosophy both as a person and as a professional. You see, we all make poor choices, some more than others. But the value of your character is measured by the level of your integrity. This is important because you're often under the microscope when working with other people's kids.

As an administrator, I found it essential to model integrity to our young staff, many of whom came directly from college. This is something most colleges don't teach their prospective teachers. As an athletic director and coach, integrity was a central component of our programs. It can be modeled, taught, and expected. I believe in winning with class and losing with honor.

Unfortunately, many of today's college and professional athletes never learned this lesson. But if you were part of our programs, then you learned how to do this. Many of you reading this message were part of those programs, and you are better people because of your integrity.

Integrity, Organization, and Ethics

I once worked for an Athletic Director/Head Football Coach who won seven state championships. As Athletic Director, his programs eventually won state championships in seven of eight men's and women's sports over the years. He was definitely my first mentor.

His first lesson to me involved integrity, organization, and ethics. He would say, "All the rest: talent, knowledge, and skill, come after these three things."

My interpretation of this statement was: do the right things first. You can always develop the other basic needs once you've established character and commitment. But if you choose to win at all costs from the beginning, then the risk of failure is much greater.

Treat Everyone With Mutual Respect

It seems like everywhere I go with my family; I run into someone I worked with, coached, or taught. My kids are always amazed at how many people stop us in public to shake my hand, give me a hug, or share a memory.

After a few times, my wife and kids just roll their eyes and shake their heads. They've asked me many times, "Can't we go anywhere without someone knowing you?" I just laugh and play it off! I explain to them that relationships are forever.

Don't get me wrong, I've made my share of enemies along the way. But when you treat everyone with mutual respect and maintain unquestionable expectations, there's always room for mutual understanding and concern.

Character—Never Let Them Quit

Muhammad Ali was the greatest boxer to ever live. He spent the last half of his life in peace and came to recognize that everyone loses along the way. It's how you handle getting knocked down which matters.

Many of you who played or coached with me over the years experienced losses. The true measure of a team or player is how you get up and go back to work. My approach was always about making progress and learning from our mistakes. Get up, dust off your pants, and move forward.

Hold Onto Your Character

Teddy Roosevelt was right on target with his idea of self-perception. Don't be driven or influenced by what others think of you. Rely on your integrity and the character you've developed.

This is important because you have to look yourself in the mirror and answer to your inner voice. When I was an AD and head football coach, we lost our high school principal during the summer. At the time, my direct supervisor was the superintendent. I had worked closely with the principal, and we were good friends. His loss was a big one for me.

Several weeks later, the district announced the hiring of a new high school principal. I wasn't involved in the hiring, but I did know the individual somewhat, he was the principal at a rival school on our schedule. He came in with guns blazing and began turning the school structure upside down. Let's just say he became very unpopular with the staff.

I heard the noise and complaints, but I stayed out of it because our fall seasons had started. I was extremely busy and didn't want to get involved in politics. After the season, the superintendent made me aware of the dissent and negativity among the high school staff. I tried to downplay it, hoping to stay out of it.

Then he leaned in and gave me a directive: "Coach, I want you to forge a relationship with our new high school principal. Get close to him and help him understand the players on staff. Try to slow him down with the changes and emphasize the need for patience."

So that's exactly what I did over the next several weeks. Once he trusted me, the principal began to take my advice, showing more tolerance and patience. By January, academic programs were beginning to show progress.

In the middle of January, I was the administrator in charge at a home basketball game when the superintendent showed up and asked to speak with me in private. We walked down the block to the stadium. In the middle of the road, he stopped and began his speech. He told me he was firing the principal by not renewing his contract for the next year.

I was shocked and asked why. He told me simply that he didn't like him and it was time for him to go. I explained that the principal was listening to me and making progress. He told me it was too late and that I needed to get out of the way.

At that point, I was upset, and my inner voice strongly urged me to speak up. I told the superintendent that the principal was now my friend and colleague, and I had done exactly as directed. There was no way in hell I was going to get out of the way.

I told him I believed he was making a mistake; one he would regret. As I walked away, I let him know I would never support his decision. I knew my actions that night would be costly, but my spirit felt betrayed.

Professional Concern and Attention

The role of a great educator definitely includes empathy, listening, and understanding. You cannot be an effective leader of young men and women without concern for their mental well-being. I'm not advocating for personal involvement or the exclusion of parental control. However, I am encouraging professional concern and attention. Pay attention to those under your influence, and notice changes in attitude and behavior. If you're uncomfortable with what might be happening with a student, utilize the resources available through administration and counseling services. Just be careful not to violate the student's basic instincts of trust. You want to be helpful, not hurtful. Remember, professional responsibilities do legally outweigh the individual needs of the student, especially in cases of suspected or ongoing abuse.

Concern Is Caring

This lesson pertains to your role as the leader. It's your program, and your goal is to teach confidence, character, commitment, and concern to all. First, you model them. Then, you insist on them from everyone under your influence. To change a program's culture, the leader should listen to all concerns but never deviate from their objectives. The measure of a leader's strength is their commitment to their character.

Concern and Passion

I've never been accused of being an overly affectionate leader, nor have many of you seen me wear my emotions on my sleeve. But many of you have learned from me how to show concern for others in your lives, including teammates, coaches, teachers, and parents.

Concern implies a troubled state of mind due to personal interest, connection, or affection. It is one of the four elements I believe must be developed in a program to effect true cultural change. Over 40 years, I taught this element by example and encouragement. I tried to share my courage and love with each participant within my influence.

1 Corinthians 13 says:

"Love is patient, love is kind. It does not envy, it does not boast, it is not proud. It does not dishonor others, it is not self-seeking, it is not easily angered, it keeps no record of wrongs. Love does not delight in evil but rejoices with the truth."

This scripture represents my version of the courage and love I tried to share and impart. The Lord knows I was far from perfect, and I asked for forgiveness often. But I never lost focus on the impact I could have on others. My efforts were always heartfelt and genuine.

A Simple Gesture Goes a Long Way

This lesson is imperative for all leaders who work with a variety of personalities each day. We all face adversities and challenges in life that we manage in our own ways. Be alert and trust your intuition about the needs of others around you. A simple gesture on your part could mean everything to someone struggling silently. You don't have to accept excuses, but you can show compassion.

Concern—The Team-First Concept

As a head coach, this was one of the hardest lessons to teach. Each player must work, commit, and self-evaluate. Then, they must be able to set aside personal accolades and achievements for the success of the team. When the team does well and wins, recognition will follow. Coaches and players quickly recognize when someone is in it only for themselves. Most sports are focused on *we*, not *me*. You win together and lose together.

Initiate Camaraderie

As an administrator, athletic director, and head coach, the attention you give to staff and team camaraderie and ownership is critical to success. The group must share common goals, similar perspectives, and loyalty to one another. Without this mutual commitment, achieving lasting success is nearly impossible. The leader's role is to initiate, guide, and model this camaraderie for all.

Commitment Includes Work and Effort

No matter how talented you are, you CANNOT replace hard work! As a coach, I refused to include a player who couldn't or wouldn't practice. To do so would send the wrong message to our team and coaching staff. Talent is God-given, but the ability to use it effectively requires practice and effort.

Nobody Is Perfect, But Effort Counts

As a leader, you usually function from the front of the pack. Being a professional educator gives you the opportunity to lead by example. Over the years, I grew accustomed to this role. My awareness of my own limitations and mistakes kept me cautious in daily decisions and actions. I openly admit that I made my share of mistakes, I'm human. The key is to learn from them and avoid repeating them. Most staff, parents, and participants will tell you there was never a doubt about my concern and commitment.

Practice Makes Progress

If you aspire to be part of a great team, then hard work, skill development, and a passion for the game are essential. You can have all the talent in the world, but a lack of commitment to those traits can limit your playing time. Coaches emphasize that practice makes perfect. Though perfection is rarely attained, it allows players and teams to grow and improve.

Reflect on the Past, Influence the Future

As I continue to lose friends and family in the second half of my life, I believe each of them played a significant role in my journey. They are missed, and I'm convinced I will see them again when my time comes.

Through my roles as an administrator, teacher, and coach, I've helped shape many young men and women in the areas of confidence, character, commitment, and concern. They have witnessed my faith and dedication firsthand. I hope they carry a part of my example with them as they move through their own lives.

PROFESSIONAL GROWTH

Be a Warrior

I learned this lesson early in my career. When I use the term *warrior* while building a program, it's a reference to the strength and courage needed to overcome adversity. I encourage participants to develop a set of values and characteristics that support their commitment to excellence. It's essential that they have confidence in their abilities while remaining devoted to the strength of the group. The success of the group is interconnected, and driven, by the efforts of its warriors.

Genuinely Forgive, Never Forget

Wow! This lesson is about doing more with less. I've had the privilege of working in some incredible school districts with outstanding facilities. At these schools, success is expected. Their teachers and coaches receive both financial resources and the equipment necessary for academic and extracurricular success. The greatest challenge there is often motivating students to consistently achieve at the highest level.

I've also worked in some of the poorest school districts in the state. In these schools, student performance was often below acceptable levels. Financial support for supplies and equipment was minimal. Unfortunately, the lack of resources sometimes became a crutch or an excuse. My philosophy has always been that *all* kids can learn and excel, despite the circumstances. Yes, the challenge is greater, but the reward is even more powerful.

I once taught a class of 28 African American World History students who had already failed the required TAKS test twice. Since they were only allowed three attempts before losing course credit, I took on the challenge. In the end, all but one passed. Fifteen of them scored in the top 3% of all test takers. It's proof that students can succeed from any background. It just takes determination, effort, and strategy from *you*, the leader. You must believe in them and put in the work, using creativity as your fuel.

Be Your Best, Never Be Less

What kind of educator are you? We each bring our own attributes and personalities to the job. There is no single "correct" way to be an effective leader. Some educators are calm, collected, and soft-spoken with a quiet strength. Others (like me) are vocal, intense, and driven by extreme commitment.

My advice: be yourself. Hold on to the traits that make you confident and effective. Don't let others sway your thoughts, ideas, or actions. A true educational leader is an influencer, a difference-maker. It's okay if others see you a little differently, as long as they are respectful and tolerant. Just be the best version of yourself.

I will not apologize for my strength and the way it intimidates you.

I will not tame my spirit and the way it howls.

I will not be less.

-L.E. Bowman

Be the Emotional Rock

A good teacher or coach must believe in their students and be there to lift them up during their lowest moments. You'll need to do the same for your students, and for your fellow teachers, administrators, and coaches. Emotionally and spiritually, it can be draining, but it's absolutely worth it if your goal is to change the culture.

If there's any doubt about your commitment, then leadership might not be your path. I've been a leader since a young age, often leaning on my faith and inner voice for strength and guidance. As you grow in your role, expect to be called upon to make that same kind of commitment.

Commitment and Dedication

What kind of educator do you want to be? Many teacher-coaches show up, execute the plan, attend the meetings, then beat the students to the parking lot. I call those professionals "custodians", they work for the paycheck.

I was never that kind of educator. I was often the first one in the building and the last one out. I tutored and met with students before school, taught my classes, ate lunch with the kids, ran afternoon practices, and stayed late for tutoring, all for little to no extra compensation. I refer to educators like that as *investment professionals*. Many of my former students and athletes can attest to this.

My goal was always to help each and every student find success within themselves. As the illustration below says: leave footprints that last a lifetime.

Many people will walk into your life, only special ones leave- footprints.

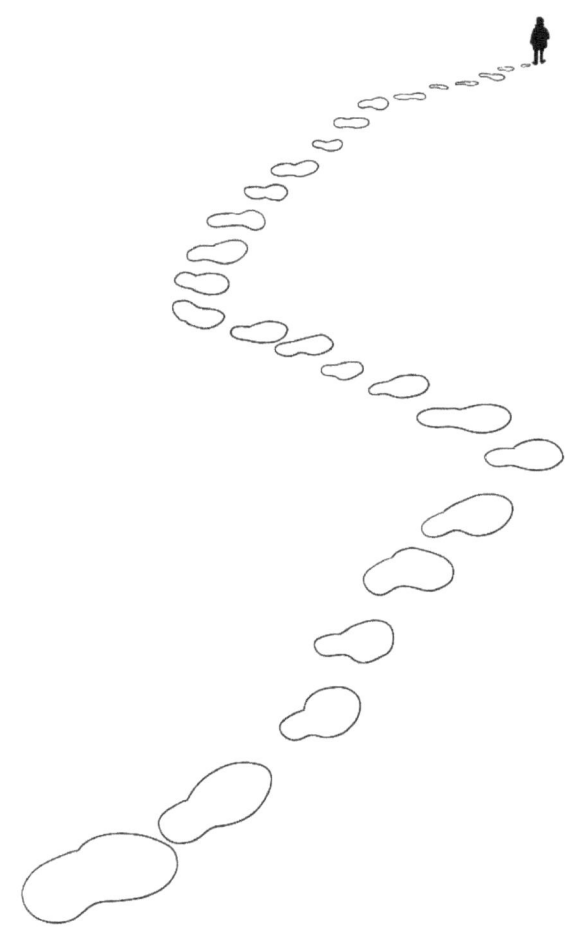

Experience Is Valuable

If you're a young administrator, teacher, or coach, never underestimate the value of experience. I was the youngest graduate assistant at the Division I level at 20 years old. By 23, I was a varsity position coach working with a Parade All-American. By 24, I was the youngest defensive coordinator at a 4A or 5A high school. At 26, I became the youngest Athletic Director and Head Football Coach at a 4A or 5A high school.

I don't share this to brag. I share it to highlight the benefits and costs of early experience. I gained a lot at a young age, but I also made mistakes. In hindsight, I would have been an even better AD and head coach later in life had I been more patient.

So, to all the young teachers and coaches out there: be patient. Learn from your mistakes. Prepare yourself so that when your moment comes, you're truly ready.

Learn From Your Past Experiences

As an administrator, teacher, and coach for 40 years, I had no choice but to learn from my past. I grew up in a very poor neighborhood in the woods of southeast Texas. Looking back, I realize the culture I came from was limiting and often negative. But I used my intelligence and athletic talent to get into college. I was a first-generation college graduate who went on to earn a master's degree early in my career.

These early life experiences taught me that life is what you make of it. I wanted to build a life and career that were exemplary and honoring to the Lord. Although I am far from perfect and have made my share of mistakes, my spirit and commitment remained strong. My passion became leading those I influenced to adopt the same values and dedication needed to build a good life. I always tried to highlight the opportunities available in the world and encouraged my students to live positively and productively.

Many of you reading this have been under my leadership, and I want you to know how proud I am that you are out there, living your lives with purpose.

We are not given a good life or a bad life.
We are given a life.
It is up to us to make it good or bad.

-Ward Foley.

Competitive Respect and Anticipation

This section is about the competitive spirit that defines both life and profession. Even Shaquille O'Neal had a worthy rival in Tim Duncan of the San Antonio Spurs. I wouldn't call it hatred. "Professional respect and anticipation" are better terms. Both were champions who competed fiercely, especially in the playoffs. Neither backed down.

As a young coach, you'll face challenges like these, too. Early in my career, I was a defensive coordinator preparing for a preseason scrimmage. The opposing head coach called his own offensive plays. Both teams had agreed to a limited number of plays per drive. On the bus ride over, my head coach told me to stay basic with our defense, don't reveal too much.

They got the ball first. On the fourth play, they broke a run for a touchdown. Their entire team, including coaches, ran down to the end zone in celebration. It was excessive, like they had just won the Super Bowl. They still had 16 more plays. On their 20th and final play, they scored again. Another wild celebration followed.

My head coach was furious. He turned to me and asked, "Can we stop them?" I replied, "Not if we stay in base defense." He told me to make adjustments during our possession. We scored twice on our 20 plays to tie it 2–2. Then he said, "Put it on these arrogant pricks!"

For the next two hours, they ran 64 plays, and we held them to zero first downs and just 50 total yards. We won the scrimmage 6–2.

Near the end, their head coach was livid. After one of our defenders made a tackle for a loss, he stormed over and shouted in my face, "This is my house, my rules, we f***ing finish when I say we do!" He was chewing tobacco, and the spit sprayed all over my face. I wiped it off and got in his face, letting him know he'd regret disrespecting me like that in front of everyone. He ran four more plays, and we shut them down cold.

That man became my nemesis for most of my career. A few years later, I took my first head coaching job, his school was in the same district. They had dominated us for decades. Within a few years, we were dominating them in every sport. Every contest became a battle. As athletic director, I brought that same fire and demanded that all our coaches and players compete with pride and command respect.

I've had several other rivalries in my career, but I'll save those stories for another time. Just remember: **Respect is a two-way street, and it should never be rooted in hate.**

Don't Be Afraid To Change The Routine

When I was a young head football coach, we were scheduled to play the #2 team in San Antonio. We were a three-touchdown underdog. The game was held at their multi-sport stadium on a Thursday night. To make matters worse, they had beaten us by 17 points the year before.

After our Wednesday night practice, I fired up our players and coaches with a passionate speech. At the end, I made an announcement: we would complete our pregame routine, including dressing out, warming up, and stretching, at our own stadium. Then, already hot and sweaty and fully suited in helmets and uniforms, we would load the buses for the 15-minute drive to their stadium. Once there, we'd jog in single-file onto the field, take off our helmets and place them under our right arms, stand for the national anthem, bow our heads for the stadium prayer, then strap up and go kick some tail. I wanted to eliminate distractions and prevent the other team from intimidating us.

The pregame atmosphere was expected to be a circus, with coverage from all the major TV affiliates (NBC, CBS, ABC). Changing our routine was my way of removing the drama. I told the players, "They have to put their pads on the same way we do."

On game day, I met with the principal, cheerleading sponsor, and band director to give them a heads-up. The principal gave me full control over team prep, and I asked the others to stick to their normal schedule. I also called the head referee to explain my plan and requested confidentiality. He agreed and said we could address any concerns when we arrived.

I mapped out every minute of our schedule leading up to our stadium arrival and posted it for everyone. We stayed on track. We boarded the buses in full uniform, in complete silence, and arrived just as both school songs were playing. We jogged onto the field in single file, helmets under our arms for the anthem, bowed for the prayer, then captains met at midfield. We won the toss and chose to receive. After returning the kickoff, our offense marched down and scored quickly.

From there, we never let up, we ran them out of their own stadium. Final score: 38–6. We had more heart than they did.

Our star running back had 28 carries for 238 yards and four touchdowns. After the game, reporters lined up to interview him. Before he spoke, I pulled him aside and said, "I'm not going to tell you what to say, but you better mention your offensive line and teammates. And show humility when they ask about our opponents, remember how we felt last year when they kicked our butt." He handled the interviews like a pro.

We beat a team that was better than us, because we wanted it more.

It's not about who is more talented.

It's about who is more hungry.

Believe in the Value of Teamwork

Create an environment that emphasizes teamwork. Encouragement and determination from others often push individuals to reach greater heights. While one person may give a good effort on their own, the power of the group can elevate them to extraordinary achievements. Inspiration from teammates build a sense of commitment and care. A good leader understands the importance of peer support and involvement.

Teach With Responsibility in Mind

This is a reminder to all of us who make a living shaping young minds. Their perceptions and attitudes are directly influenced by those entrusted with their care. Let's also remember that parents have rights and expectations, and we must respect that.

It's not that our passion or insistence is wrong; we are inherently responsible for students while they are in our care. Every mind is capable of learning. We must teach in ways that meet individual needs. A gifted mind learns differently than one with special needs. Let's remain reasonable and avoid pushing a one-size-fits-all approach.

Be Inspirational

Inspiration is the enthusiasm sparked by someone or something that leads to new ideas or motivation. A good leader considers how to inspire students or athletes during planning and organizing. With clear objectives and strategies, a leader must lead with energy and purpose.

Your role as an influencer matters. Some days and lessons will be tougher than others, but that's when it's most important to go the extra mile to engage the kids.

Exemplify Strength and Courage

Courage is defined as the mental or moral strength to venture, persevere, and withstand danger, fear, or difficulty. If you are a young teacher or coach, you should realize it takes a great deal of courage to perform your job successfully. As an administrator, educational leader, and influencer, I always understood that my role demanded strength and courage. I was the instrument of cultural change within a program. It was imperative that I set the example and demonstrate the direction needed. That's the interesting aspect of courage: once you display it consistently, it becomes contagious for the community and participants.

Be Strong and Resilient

If you're still following, then you know my respect for your jobs and careers is genuine. I pray for all of you daily, and I'm specific about your needs and situations. I usually end my prayers with a request: I ask God to strengthen each of you, for He promises us strength in **Isaiah 40:29–30**. This promise will guide and comfort you through the trials and tribulations of your daily routine. I share these prayers because I know many believers prayed for me during my own walk.

Be Diligent and Determined

As a head football coach, I once worked for a principal whom I believed to be devious and manipulative. After my first semester at that school, I began assembling a respected and knowledgeable coaching staff. Most public schools require coaches to also teach, so I worked to secure qualified staff who could fulfill both roles.

After a few months, as I was finalizing staff changes to support our athletic program's goals, I discovered the principal and head counselor had manipulated the student scheduling numbers. They presented data designed to eliminate the teaching slots of two departing coaches, an intentional act to block their replacements. The numbers were fabricated and didn't reflect actual faculty needs.

I received this information confidentially and brought my concerns to the superintendent. He gave me permission to approach other campus principals and offered to transfer teaching units to their schools if they were willing to hire the coaches I recommended. Fortunately, a few principals were receptive, and we quietly moved forward with interviews and placements.

A few days later, the principal, head counselor, and a vice principal called me into a meeting to inform me, regretfully, of the "elimination" of the teaching positions. Little did they know, I had already secured the slots through the superintendent.

Several weeks later, the high school principal met with the superintendent and admitted they had "made a mistake" in their numbers and now needed those teacher units back. The superintendent told him it was too late; the positions had already been reassigned to other campuses.

This caused quite a stir, as the History and English departments ended up with a 40:1 student-to-teacher ratio. It was the consequence of his deceitful manipulation. Honestly, I felt bad for him, he had no idea how formidable I could be when pushed. Let's just say he never underestimated me again.

Be Persistent

Persistence and determination define the mindset necessary for progress. You'll notice I didn't mention "permission." Politics and procedures often require leaders to seek approval before taking action. But as an agent of change, I found it more effective to act with clear expectations and objectives in mind.

I rarely asked for permission unless absolutely necessary. Sometimes I knew the answer would be "no," so I always had a backup plan. My philosophy was simple: it's easier to ask for forgiveness than to ask for permission. I will caution you; this mindset might put you in the crosshairs of job security. But my attitude was always, "I was looking for a job when I got this one, so do your best and don't sweat the rest."

Reliability and Persistence

As an educational leader, it's understood that you are the decision-maker. Most young teachers and coaches take the job with great intentions and ideas. However, most colleges and certification programs don't prepare you for dealing with critics.

When you're working with people's children, respect from parents and community members isn't guaranteed. Some people will believe they know more than you, can coach or teach better than you, and can make better decisions than you. I call these individuals "critics."

They'll speak negatively about you to their kids, to any staff who will listen, and to community members. Yet, few will ever approach you directly. I view these critics as lost souls. I pray for them, but I don't let them consume my energy. Instead, I focus on the participants I serve. Build strong, trusting relationships with them. They are your saving grace. Their success and growth will often silence and discredit even your harshest critics.

Be Influential

Influence is the capacity to have an effect on the character, development, or behavior of someone or something, especially without using force or coercion. As an educational leader, my goal was always to effect positive change through encouragement, structure, and determination.

If you've read this far, then you know how much influence you hold over your staff, community, and participants. My advice: use that influence to move your program forward in a constructive and meaningful way. Remember, **you set the table for the entire meal of success**.

Be Decisive

All good educational leaders find themselves in the position of being the decision-maker for their program. A decision is, in fact, the act of making up one's mind about a situation or issue. How you arrive at that final decision can vary based on circumstances, facts, implications, and consequences. It should never be made out of anger or influenced by politics. Some leaders take time to contemplate and patiently weigh the issue. Those who know me well can attest that this was not my style. As an administrator, teacher, and coach, my time was valuable. So, I became astute at listening, evaluating, and then making a decision quickly. My focus remained on doing the right thing, and then moving on to the next situation.

Be a Disciplinarian

I never understood the animosity and negative perceptions some parents had when I disciplined their child. If you are a teacher or coach, realize that discipline is a major component of managing expectations and performance. You must establish program rules and guidelines along with appropriate consequences for violations. This is where fairness and consistency are essential to team building and morale. Most parents support and sign your rules, but some won't be supportive when it comes to their own child. Always remember: the rules are for everyone in your organization or team. The disapproving parent always has a choice, their child abides by the same rules as everyone else, or they can choose to participate elsewhere. Participation is not a right; it's a privilege.

Build Lifetime Relationships

Did you know that teaching and coaching young people actually requires strategies that develop both their academic and emotional needs? It's true that our professional focus is on program success and advancement, but many of those successes depend on our ability to foster a positive self-perception and emotional stability in the participants we influence. This requires establishing trusting and secure relationships with them. I believe we have the ability to teach confidence, character, commitment, and compassion: not just to students, but to all we work with. These are life skills that help people become better human beings.

Be Humble and Selfless

This applies to all educators. Most of the time, your devotion and commitment to your job are not reciprocated. They're sometimes appreciated, but rarely recognized. You are in the business of encouraging, learning and enhancing the lives of those you serve. It's a humbling and fulfilling experience, and it should never be about the accolades. Rest assured: your efforts are enough, and your good deeds will have lasting impact. Never doubt it, kids always remember the best teachers and coaches. They rarely forget the worst, except in disgust or as a joke. Love what you do, and do what you love.

Be Forgiving, But Don't Forget

Over the years, I've had personal and professional relationships that I realized were not good for me. Most people are inherently self-preserving, so you become expendable when their needs change. I learned this the hard way as a young man. The toughest lesson was learning how to forgive, heal, and move on. Later in life, I found it necessary to release the hurt and resentment. Letting go is part of spiritual and emotional growth, and your health depends on it. If you're young and making your way through life, know this: forgiveness is important, but that doesn't mean you have to forget. Remembering teaches you, protects you, and ultimately makes you stronger.

Maintain a Positive Attitude

If you think you can, if you know they can, if you sincerely believe they can, then your positive attitude and commitment will find a way to get you all there. As a leader of change, you must rely on determination and the power of positive reinforcement. Programs that need turning around often carry years of negative experiences. Many participants have lost faith and fallen into the habit of making excuses. The administration, community, and students hope for a new start with your arrival, though some may harbor doubts. You need to hit the ground running with a competent plan in hand. Your attitude must exude confidence, commitment, and concern. In my experience, these are the qualities that erase the past and build the future.

Don't Forget to Laugh

This is one of my favorite perspectives! As educators, we often get caught up in the demands of the job. If you're one of those people (as I always was), then don't forget to dream. Holding on to the positive outcomes of your work helps you see the potential that others might miss. The job requires you to be firm and assertive with your directions and expectations, but don't lose sight of the dream. And because the job is demanding, take every chance to laugh. Don't underestimate the power of laughter, it lightens the pressure in tense moments. Working with kids provides plenty of opportunities to laugh and shake your head. Allow yourself those moments.

Take Care of Your Own Needs

I got this important illustration from a young educator who once played for me. He's a great young man and a fine teacher/coach. It's a reflection of the dedication and awareness most educators possess. Take a lesson from me: you must make an effort to take care of yourself because your needs count too. It's important to be attentive and devoted to the kids while also being realistic about your own well-being. A good educator learns how to pace themselves.

Acknowledge and Respect Your Work Stress

It's important that you pay attention to certain physical and emotional reactions to stressful situations. If you follow my writing at all, then you'll recognize my approach to handling these reactions, drawn from 40 years of a successful career. I've described a similar breathing technique before, but one key part is often left out: say a little prayer and let your inner voice guide you through.

I will breathe.

I will think of solutions.

I will not let my stress levels break me.

I will not let my stress level break me.

I will simply breathe.

And it will be okay.

Because I don't quit.

Managing Your Stress

There is a problem among educational staff in this state. So many of us (myself included) willingly give too much of our time, concern, and emotion to our jobs and communities. At the height of my career, it was normal for me to put in 90–100 hours a week supervising, directing, and preparing our programs. Heck, I worked through the wee hours of the night and sometimes even slept at the field house just to get a couple of extra hours of rest.

That lifestyle eventually caught up with me. I developed early-onset symptoms of a couple of diseases, illnesses that were both permanent and preventable. Physical and emotional stress were major contributing factors. I had to learn how to manage the stress and reduce my hours. After shifting my mindset, I went on to enjoy 25 more years of a successful and productive career. My advice to young educators is to remain passionate and devoted, but practice it with a healthy dose of moderation.

Be Calm and Collected

This is a lesson in anger management for young teachers and coaches. As the leader of your domain, you will have many opportunities to address inappropriate behaviors, both from students and their parents. I include parents because many student misbehaviors reflect their home environments in one way or another.

I want to caution you about how you respond in these situations. The natural reaction is often to get angry at the student, but you should strive to be better than that. Some students act out specifically to get under your skin. I learned the hard way that anger is a form of affirmation for some of them, because that's what they're used to seeing at home. Ignoring such behavior can sometimes escalate it.

So, take a deep breath, and try to redirect the student with a relevant question about the lesson or activity. If that doesn't work, ask them to gather their things and move to a seat closer to the door, then continue teaching as if nothing happened. If that still doesn't work, pause the class, walk to the door, and ask them to step outside. Instruct them to remain by the door without leaving. Then return to class and refocus your students on an activity.

Once the class is engaged, step outside and calmly have a conversation about expectations. That cooling-off period usually helps and gives the student time to reflect. Come to an agreement about what behavior would have been more appropriate. If needed, send the student to the office with a referral.

Always keep your cool. Be assertive, but never angry. Anger is never a good answer to a negative situation.

Choices made in anger
can ruin your life.

Talent Evaluation

When working with kids, they come in all shapes, sizes, and abilities. I believe in opportunity for all, and talent sometimes comes in small packages of dynamite. I don't think you can ever underestimate determination and guts. But occasionally, unfortunate circumstances arise where this is not the case.

As a head football coach, I once had a tremendously talented 105 lb. defensive back. We were a 5A established program with some very strong, large, and talented players. This little defensive back held his own with some of them as a 9th and 10th grader. But he didn't grow anymore. So, the summer before his junior year, I had a conference with him and his parents. I let them know that I had made a decision about his involvement in our football program. I could not, in good conscience, allow him to play anymore because I feared for his physical safety. I offered him several other roles within our athletic programs, but he would not be suiting up with us in the fall.

He and his parents were very upset, so they decided to make an appeal with our superintendent. We had a conference in his office with all of us present. The superintendent heard my concerns and then listened to the parents' appeal for him to overturn my decision. At the end of the meeting, the superintendent promised to make his decision within a week.

A few days later, the major metropolitan newspaper published a front-page story about one of my players: a 6'8", 270-pound tight end who was a National Merit Scholar. It was a great article about an outstanding young man who had just signed to play at Princeton University. The day the article came out, I received a morning phone call from the superintendent, commending the news coverage and wanting to personally meet the young man. So, we set up an appointment for that afternoon, and I got permission from his mom to take him over to the central office.

I picked him up, and we went to see the superintendent. When we got outside his office door, his secretary buzzed to let him know we had arrived. He opened his door, looked up, and his jaw dropped in disbelief at how big the tight end was. He shook our hands and invited us into his office. He spent about 10 minutes getting to know the kid and telling him how proud he was. Afterwards, he asked the player to step outside for a minute while we discussed something. So, he stepped out and sat down.

The conversation quickly turned to the little defensive back who had appealed my decision. The superintendent raised his voice slightly and accused me of setting him up. I replied that there was no way he would ever agree to let the little guy get hit by someone as big as the tight end. I laughed and reminded him that he had requested to meet the tight end. Then I took the opportunity to let him know that we had at least five other players who were even bigger. He shook his head in agreement, acknowledging that I had made a valid point. The next day, he called the boy's parents to inform them that he would support my decision.

A few weeks later, the young man and his parents withdrew him from our school entirely. It turned out that they enrolled him in a jockey training school at the Retama Horse Racing Track. Ten years later, a few coaches from that staff and I met at Oaklawn Horse Racing Track in Arkansas to watch the final day's racing card. We got to watch that same young man win the Arkansas Derby, and he became the jockey champion for the season, meaning he won more races than any of the other 15 professional jockeys during the meet.

Later that day, we had dinner with him and his wife. We all congratulated him on finding his passion in life. In the end, he admitted he had been very upset when I had to cut him, but he thanked me because it ultimately led him down a better path. Sometimes, decisions work out for the best, and this was one of those times.

Don't Be a Critic, Be a Supporter

Over the past four decades, I've learned a lot of lessons. One of the best is knowing the difference between being a critic and being a supporter of a participant's performance. Many of my writings mention the importance of positive reinforcement while working with kids. It's a building block for instilling confidence and commitment.

Grading and evaluating performance are a necessary step in correcting mistakes and further developing skills. It can be intense and pointed, but never personal. Once this process is completed, encouragement and positive reinforcement techniques should be used to help the participant improve.

Participation Trophies and Ribbons

This topic should be important to young teachers and coaches across the country. For most, success does not come easy. In this world where everyone gets a participation trophy or ribbon, we're not teaching our children the value of competition and the spirit of hard work.

We now have an entire generation of young people who think success is about showing up and announcing, "I'm here." They fold when they discover it's really about sacrifice, perseverance, long hours, and passion. It seems that many from the younger generation will have to learn this lesson the hard way.

As an educator, you'll likely find yourself helping these participants grow while learning this lesson.

Carefully Contemplate Your Opportunities

If you are an administrator, teacher, or coach, gaining experience and building a career is always a consideration. Usually, your main focus is educating and developing kids. This is your passion, and your top priority is making a difference in the lives within your influence. Your dedication and commitment will be noticed, and this recognition often leads to more and better opportunities along the way.

Be advised that you will likely need to consider new job opportunities as you advance your career. Making a change to another school or district should always be evaluated seriously. The toughest part of these decisions is often leaving behind the kids and the community you've grown committed to. My advice is simple: career decisions should never be based solely on the emotions of leaving. Every district, school, and program have students who will benefit from your service and passion. Your decision should be based on a serious opportunity to move up, consider factors like facility quality, administrative support, and relationship familiarity.

I'll leave you with one thought: remember, the grass is not always greener on the other side of the fence, it's just different grass. If you're going to move, do it with a purpose.

All Jobs Are Not Equal

To every young educator wondering about their opportunities for advancement: there are a few criteria you can control in this process. Many of you have been advised or mentored by someone you respect and admire. Most of these mentors emphasize the importance of the program's success and reputation, academics, achievements, facilities, socioeconomic factors, and the broader community. These elements often provide a better platform for professional success and are considered one of the best ways to build a career.

When you start talking with mentors about students, they'll tell you there are kids everywhere who need your help. For me, I see it a bit differently. My first teaching and coaching job was at a high school on Kelly Air Force Base in San Antonio, Texas. We had strong academics and great athletic programs. For four years, I had the privilege of coaching some of the best athletes anywhere. My career started off with a bang, and I got exposure to great coaches I could learn from.

Man, I soaked it up, handling equipment, laundry, fieldhouse cleanup, play cards, and managing our scouting program and schedules. I dealt with a lot of organizational tasks while learning the coaching skills of my trade. That was the first step toward advancing to the next level.

The second step was furthering my education, I earned a master's degree in school administration, but there are many options to explore. The third step was networking with peers through conferences and coaching clinics. The more people you know, the more your name gets recognized in teaching and coaching circles. Step four? Keep your résumé updated.

Let's talk about job opportunities. While my first job was a great professional experience, I realized that most of the jobs I was qualified for didn't fit neatly into that same mold. I started applying for every football coordinator job within a 100-mile radius. I was 24 years old and only got four interviews. I received one offer, from a 3A school that hadn't won a game in three years.

When I got there, the athletes were mostly average, and they had a poor attitude about playing and winning. The district was the poorest in the state in capital per student, and the student body was majority minority. Our first year, we weren't very good. But in the second year, my defense led the league in yards allowed and turnovers.

The decision to go to that school went against all conventional wisdom about how to advance your career. But two years later, I was hired as an athletic director and head football coach, at the age of 26. It was a similar type of school district. Three years into that job, we won the first district championship in the school's history.

One last thought: all kids are not the same. Students from poorer economic backgrounds often live by different cultural norms than those in middle- and upper-class communities. So, you'll have to decide how you want your advancement to count.

INNER CIRCLE

Create An Inner Circle

In my observations, I often refer to an inner circle when changing and building a program. It is a small group of people within a larger group who have insight on program direction, influence, and objectives. An inner circle serves as a guiding force for staff, community, and participants. Their roles are recognized and respected by all within a program. The educational leader is dependent on their ideas, support, and loyalty. His selection of the inner circle members is crucial to the progress and success of the program. The members should be diverse in education, experience, and knowledge while sharing common characteristics and objectives. Their support and loyalty are a must when contributing to program advancements.

It's not about the circle.

It's about the loyalty in it.

Inner Circle Selection – Expectations

As you are choosing your inner circle, a good leader must lean on them to maximize his performance. This circle is essential to the achievement process. Each member has earned their role and carved out their place in the circle. They could and should be different from one another, for each brings their own talents, intellect, and insights. The leader must be accepting and flexible in his dealings with each, and he must deal with all in equality and fairness. Some inner circle members will leave, and others will join the circle as time dictates. All members must be supportive, honest, committed, and loyal. Otherwise, they must be asked to leave the circle!

Accept people as they are, but place them where they belong. You are the CEO of your life. Hire, fire, and promote accordingly.

Assess and Utilize Their Strengths

It's important to realize that there are some people in this world who find their way to your inner circle. When they show up with good intentions, try to remember that our world is smaller than you think. Utilize your instincts and inner voice in deciding their place and contribution within the circle. Accomplishments are less likely to be realized without the input and help from others. Connections are lasting when you rely on one another to get things done.

A good leader will always develop and nurture lasting relationships.

Hiring Staff, Set Aside Friendships

I am so grateful to have worked with some outstanding professionals in my long career! As a leader, I learned early on to value those who shared a common philosophy, work ethic, and expectations. There were some who did not, and I felt responsible to help them change or move on without them! Moving on is sometimes very difficult, but it is sometimes necessary for progress and direction!

Commit to Your Staff, Be Present

As an administrator, athletic director, and head football coach, it was very important for me to support and encourage the coaches that worked with me. Their jobs were always difficult and demanding, with many of them working as classroom teachers and full-time coaches. Many of them spent more time coaching kids than they did teaching. There is a tremendous amount of pressure, preparation, and time commitment involved in assembling and developing a successful team. When I was the athletic director, I met with each head coach daily to discuss squad members, parental concerns, assistant coaches, academic performance, discipline issues, budget and transportation, and competitor results. I always ended these meetings with encouraging words and unquestioning loyalty. I hired these men and women to build successful teams, and I certainly owed them my concern and support. In return, I always got their best efforts.

[Great] Coaches carry a lot on their shoulders. Some of it you see, but a lot of it you don't see.

Every decision weighs a ton, and even when they have the best support system, it's still hard trying to clearly communicate what they are dealing with on a day-to-day basis.

So check on your coaches and make sure they are okay, and make sure they know you appreciate them.

Depend on Your Inner Circle

Which one are you? Our world is full of people who are satisfied with sitting in the stands and being critics. Then there are those who want change but are unwilling to be part of the solution. Of course, there are a few who will stand with you as agents of change. You could call them colleagues or supporters. As a leader, you will have to be very convincing to move the first two types into the last category. Be willing to gather an inner circle of support to help in this process. If the goals and expectations are positive, then you have a chance to advance your program.

Some people want it to happen.

Some wish it would happen.

Others make it happen.

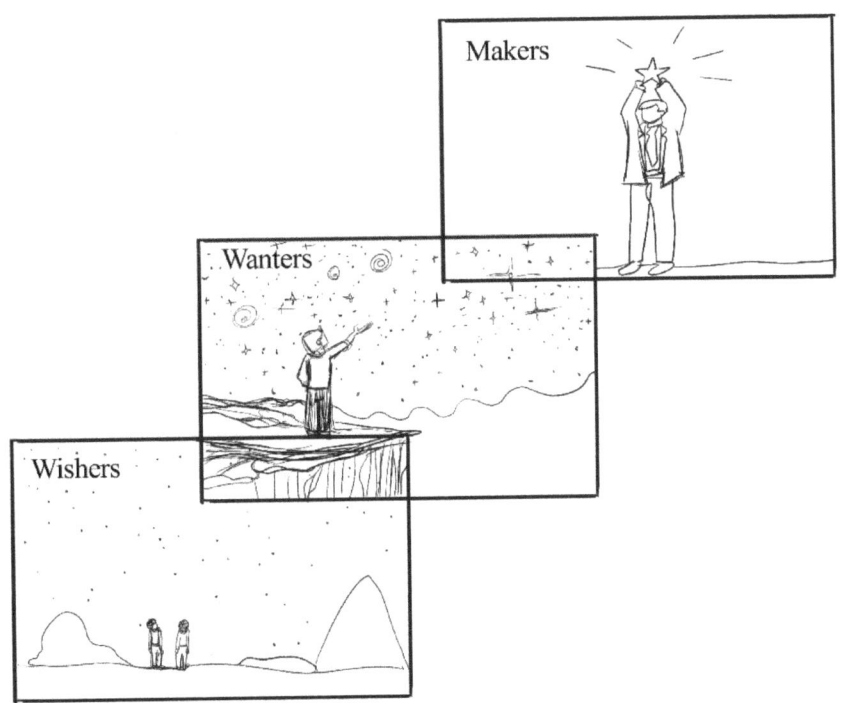

Build an Unbreakable Bond with Them

When building a program from day one, assembling a competent staff of professionals becomes quite the challenge. I always started with the idea that we all must be loyal, committed, and objectively concerned about the development of our kids. Staff needed to know that I had their back, and I needed to be confident that they had mine. This bond needed to hold up under any type of pressure. When you build a staff from these expectations, tremendous relationships and friendships emerge!

Don't walk behind me, I may not lead. Don't walk in front of me, I may not follow. Just walk beside me and be my friend.

Albert Camus.

Let Them Be Independent Thinkers

As an administrator, teacher, and coach, I was directly involved in staff selection and development. When selecting staff, the most important characteristic I looked for was independent thinking. I wanted to hire someone who would be a willing participant in our collaborative decision-making process. In the interview process, I looked to see if the candidate was realistically grounded in their beliefs and perceptions. It's important to realize that you can teach organization and knowledge on the job. But you cannot teach work ethic, independent thinking, and a positive attitude. I was never interested in hiring an average thinker or an undisciplined and weak-minded individual. If you settle for this, then you end up compromising the basic needs of your program. So, turn on your listening skills and be sure to ask relevant questions during the interview.

Strong minds discuss ideas.
Average minds discuss events.
Weak minds discuss people.

-Socrates

Others' Ideas and Thoughts

If you can learn this lesson earlier in life, you could be a much better boss and friend down the road! It's much better to listen and collaborate than to push forward no matter what. Even if it's not in your nature, try to be open-minded and hear others' thoughts and opinions.

Took me thirty to realize that if you want to get the opportunity to be the greatest version of yourself, sometimes you got to be someone you are not to hear the voice of reason.

Expect Loyalty

When building a program as the leader, you must find people who share the same expectations and ideas. Loyalty is a sense of duty or devoted attachment to something or someone. It's very important to have when developing an inner circle. Ideas, objectives, and commitments will come from all members of your inner circle. The members must be able to share, trust, and rely on one another in the most trying, adverse, and stressful situations. It's important for the leader to insist, encourage, and eventually demand loyalty from all participants in the process of building a successful program. In closing, loyalty is not blind following. The leader must work daily on nurturing and reinforcing its boundaries within his inner circle. In other words, he must lead by example in his display of loyalty toward the members of his inner circle.

Loyalty is rare; if you find it, keep it.

Inspire and Delegate

As an administrative leader in education, it was always important for me to assemble and empower a small group of leaders called my inner circle. This circle had important input in and implementation of program objectives and direction. Their role as leaders was essential to influencing staff, parents, and participants in a positive manner. When you are the leader of a program, it's essential that your inner circle trust, respect, and exemplify your philosophy.

If you look at the people in your circle and don't get inspired, then you don't have a circle, you have a cage.

Create a Family Atmosphere

If you are one of the administrators, teachers, or coaches that I have worked with over the past 40 years, then you were witness to my attitude of family while working with you. My first coaching staff as athletic director/head football coach was a combination of both young and experienced coaches. I had that job for almost 10 years, and that staff was a collection of brothers and sisters that bonded together as a family. The job was so difficult and political that all we had was one another. We all had our faults and weaknesses, but we bonded together so well. After a few years of building confidence and character with the kids and community, we began to see incredible progress both in the athletic arena and the classroom. As far as I know, there were only two district championships won (boys' track & baseball) in over 100 years of the school district's existence. After 9 years there, our staff helped the kids raise 19 championship banners in the rafters of our gymnasium. Our athletes produced two National Merit Scholars and dozens of top 10 graduates of their senior class. As a staff, we completely reversed the negative perceptions and built success based on expectations and positive reinforcement. It was an incredible coaching staff where we would share nights out, staff BBQs, Super Bowl parties, and many successful awards ceremonies. Today, a few of them have passed, many have retired, while others have moved on to become successful superintendents, principals, and counselors. They have moved on to be influencers in their own right! But all have been, and still are, close members of my family. And there are many more out there, from other staffs, that I have served. If you are reading this post, you know who you are because we bonded at the time. I thank you for your friendship.

Family is not about blood. It's about who is willing to hold your hand when you need it the most.

Cherish Your Professional Relationships

Be advised that really great friendships are hard to find and maintain! I have been a part of 13 teaching, coaching, and administrative staffs. It should be noted that I had the opportunity to build relationships with thousands of individuals along the way. I can safely say that I can only acknowledge fewer than 30 of them as good friends. Of those, only a couple of handfuls (less than 10) would I consider my best friends forever. This is life because circumstances change and people grow apart. I think I might have 5 or 6 of them still alive today. If you are one of them (you know who you are), I am eternally grateful! My first athletic director job was challenging, as I was the youngest in the state (26 years old). The first coaching staff that I was able to assemble was the best group of professionals and people that I worked with over 40 years. There were 8 head coaches and 14 assistants. We were all good friends and close emotionally. There were 5 of them that became lifetime friends. Two of them have gained their wings and left this world, and another is to leave us any day now. The two that are left know how much I care and love them. My many good friends know the same, and some of you I have mentored, coached, and taught along the way! To you I say, I have faith in you and trust you will pay it forward as I have!

Everyone has a friend during each stage of life. But only the lucky ones have the same friend in all stages of life.

194

Have a Soulful Inner Voice

This is a revelation for me! I am realizing that each of us must strive to seek and develop the gifts that God has breathed into our souls — **Genesis 2:7**. Our soul is the spiritual essence of our being, which includes identity, personality, aptitudes, perceptions, and a reflection of our inner spirit. These soulful traits allow us to find our faith, purpose, and calling throughout life and beyond death. Each of us can seek our purpose by listening to our inner voice. For me, I found mine in working with, encouraging, and nourishing relationships with the kids within my influence.

Who you are, what your values are, what you stand for.... They are your anchor, your north star. You won't find them in a book. You'll find them in your soul.

-Anne M. Mulcahy

Enjoy Your Working Environment

This message is meant for all the staff members and players I've had the pleasure of working with at the 13 stops of my career. Despite many of the negative situations that occurred along the way, I had so much fun working with you all! We shared countless laughs, created lasting memories, and enjoyed many positive moments that I will never forget.

I have tried to stay in touch with many of you, and I value every communication we've had. You know who you are when I say this. Many of you, I've just started to track down again. Take heart when I tell you how important it was for me to serve you! My hope is that y'all are living positive, adventurous, and fun lives, just as mine has been.

Recognize and Cultivate Your Support Group

I've been through a lot during one lifetime, and I've had a lot of success along the way. It's important to acknowledge those who supported me throughout.

First and foremost is my personal relationship with the Lord. Through Him, I am only His servant. I have a beautiful and intelligent wife who has stood by me through both good and bad times. My children have always been by my side, offering strength and love.

There have been hundreds, among thousands, of teachers and coaches who fought by my side. Lastly, but never least, are all the parents and players who were supportive and devoted to excellence. Without all of these supporters, I would be just a humble man without influence.

I thank you all from the bottom of my heart and hope that I've been able to touch your lives, just as many of you have touched mine.

QUALITY LEADERSHIP

Acknowledge Your Purpose

This lesson is about purpose. If you're a young teacher or coach, you must realize by now the impact you have on kids. You are an influencer by profession, which means your relationships with young people matter. Many of them have no idea what they want to do with their lives, now or in the future. I always saw my role as a listener and a conduit for ideas. My job was to help students explore their interests while sharing my passion. I could share my story and, in doing so, encourage them to write their own. Teaching and coaching were my passions, and they became my avenue to influence. If you're in this just for a paycheck, your satisfaction will be limited. For me, it was a calling, and it was deeply rewarding.

The two most important days in your life are the day you are born and the day you find out why.

-Mark Twain

Leadership Style

What kind of leader are you? Those who have worked with me in various situations will attest to my leadership style. I can be annoying, assertive, vocal, and opinionated, but working with me usually creates a strong bond. I'm loyal, supportive, and determined. However, I have no tolerance for laziness, ignorance, or manipulation. Most people come to rely on and trust my personality and direction. But there have been a few who didn't understand or appreciate my approach. In my experience, professionals who struggle with that usually have a hard time being part of any team.

If they stand behind you, protect them.
If they stand beside you, respect them.
If they stand against you, defeat them.

Pull Back the Curtain of Darkness

When you step into a leadership role in education, your first responsibility is to assess the direction and attitude of those in the building, both staff and students. Your observations should be inclusive. Public education is a mission of academic and social progress for every student it serves. Unfortunately, many staff and community members lose sight of this mission, which is why so many schools and programs underperform. As a leader, you must pull back the curtain of darkness and bring in a beam of spiritual light and expectation. You are the agent of change. You are the beacon of light, hope, and direction for your program. You don't need permission to lead, but you do need understanding, cooperation, and teamwork. Your flicker of light should inspire hope and optimism. It all starts with you and your determination.

Hope is being able to see that there is light despite all of the darkness.

Be the Captain of Your Ship

As the educational leader, you are the captain of the ship. You are responsible for setting the tone, establishing objectives, and modeling the behavior you expect. You are both an influencer and a mentor to staff and students. I've always seen this job as both motivational and directional. They say you can lead a horse to water, but you can't make it drink. But if you ask those I've worked with, many will tell you, I can make that horse pretty thirsty! That's who I am: a leader who pushes, prods, and applies his will in a positive and empowering way.

You can't make someone be who
you want them to be

But you be who you are.

-Amanda Blair

Lead or Get Out of the Way

I'm fairly certain Dr. Patton was right about leadership. Over the years, I've worked with both exceptional and poor leaders. I learned most of what I know from the best, and a great deal of what *not* to do from the worst.

I once served as the Offensive Coordinator for a football team that went 7-2. We made it to the first round of the playoffs. That Saturday morning before the game, the Head Coach walked into the meeting room where our offensive staff was already hard at work. He told us to stop. He took over the meeting and informed us he was changing our entire offense, installing a new one tailored to our young sophomore quarterback's skills.

We were shocked. We pleaded with him to wait until spring to implement the changes, explaining that a few days simply wasn't enough time. I told him it was a mistake. He did it anyway, and we helped him put it in place.

Game night came. In the first three minutes, we had two fumbles inside our 10-yard line and an interception returned for a touchdown. We were down 21-0 before we could even regroup. By the middle of the second quarter, we still hadn't earned a first down and were trailing 28-0.

I was in the press box on the headset when the Head Coach called up, asking how we could get a first down. I started to suggest a few adjustments, but he cut me off, cursing, ripping off his headset, and storming off the field toward the locker room.

I was stunned. The receivers coach picked up the headset and asked where he went. I said, "He just left the stadium. Get the QB and put him on."

I calmed the quarterback down and asked if he and the team remembered our original offense from the regular season. He said they did. I told him we were going back to it and asked him to step up and lead.

We scored on our last two possessions of the half and went into halftime down 28-14. The locker room was buzzing with energy. Still no sign of the Head Coach. I ignored the situation and focused on the game.

We got the ball to start the second half and scored to make it 28-21. We then held them on defense and tied the game 28-28. They managed a 9-minute drive to go up 35-28. We got the ball one last time and drove into the red zone. I used all our timeouts, but we ran out of time before scoring.

We lost the game, but we made them fight for it.

Afterward, in the locker room with the players, the Head Coach finally returned. All he said was, "Get on the bus."

That Monday morning, I went into his office and resigned. I told him he was the worst leader I had ever worked with and that I was appalled by his behavior during the game.

Within two weeks, I had another job.

Every person in a leadership position is not a leader. Many times, it's not the person who holds the position that gets authentic Loua things done; it's the follower behind the scenes who is leading the orchestra.

-Dr. Patton

Development of Leadership Skills

Our colleges do not offer leadership development courses to prepare future teachers and coaches. As a teenager, I overcame serious challenges with shyness and stuttering. I became involved with my church group and participated in team sports, experiences that helped me build confidence and self-esteem. It took a lot of prayer and hard work! Eventually, I became a respected leader among my teammates and in my community.

By the time I went off to college, I was both physically and spiritually ready to face the world. After graduating and landing my first teaching and coaching job, I was determined to continue enhancing my leadership skills. Five years later, as a head coach, I made leadership development a key objective of our program.

Some people are natural-born leaders, while others grow into the role through experience and development. Still, many people do not wish to lead; they must learn instead how to be supportive, loyal followers.

Leadership is communicating to people their worth and potential so clearly that they are inspired to see it in themselves.

Have a Bright Spirit

Surround yourself with positive thinkers, people who welcome your participation in a collaborative process. A miserable spirit, on the other hand, often drains energy and discourages progress.

Even Jesus didn't give up on the negative spirits of some of His disciples when they showed signs of doubt. Instead, He showered them with love and understanding. Yet, He remained focused on the purpose for which the Father sent Him.

Let your bright spirit shine and lift those who may be struggling with doubt.

I don't care what anyone says, but you can sense a jealous spirit, negative energy, and a miserable person.

Organize and Know Your Responsibilities

Wow! When you're leading a large athletic program with 1,500 participants, you need broad shoulders. As athletic director, I eventually managed 12 head coaches and 34 assistant coaches across 14 sports. When you add in parents, booster clubs, maintenance, custodial staff, and event personnel, the scope of responsibility becomes massive.

You could say the job was all-encompassing and quite a challenge. I often felt I could never catch up. But by the grace of God, I found a way to manage it all. This was on top of parent conferences, budgeting, administrative meetings, leadership seminars, and UIL executive committee duties.

Jeremiah 29:11 became my anchor:

"'For I know the plans I have for you,' declares the Lord, 'plans to prosper you and not to harm you, plans to give you hope and a future.'"

That scripture gave me strength and determination. I worked many long nights and regularly closed the facilities myself. At the end of each day, I would pray for the strength and guidance to face the next.

Clearly, something was working, we hung 19 championship banners in our athletic facility. We helped many student-athletes earn college scholarships and nurtured young men and women who went on to become police officers, firefighters, doctors, nurses, and business professionals. I consider all of them public servants, giving back to their communities.

I ask not for a lighter burden but for broader shoulders.

Learn to Prioritize

As an educational leader, you'll face multiple situations daily, often happening all at once. Each incident, a unique action or occurrence, deserves your attention.

My advice is to pause and prioritize. Take a deep breath, say a short prayer, and proceed with each matter in order of importance. Before long, you'll clear your list, just in time to start a new one.

Often when you think you're at the end of something, you're at the beginning of something else.

-Fred Rogers

Code of Personal Conduct and Standards

It became clear to me early on that staff, players, and athletes came from various backgrounds and home lives. After careful observation, I realized there needed to be a basic code of conduct and shared expectations for personal behavior under my leadership.

In one of our early meetings, my inner circle and I agreed upon core standards of respect:

- Say "yes, sir" and "no, sir."

- Make eye contact when speaking with someone.

- Shake hands when introduced.

- Don't interrupt.

- Respond when spoken to.

- Don't speak out of anger or frustration.

- Control your temper.

- Be positive and encouraging.

- Acknowledge effort and celebrate accomplishments.

- Accept compliments graciously.

Some of these behaviors may challenge cultural norms learned at a young age. That's why it's critical that your staff understands and agrees with these standards, they will model them daily. As the leader, you must model them too. If these are your expectations, then you must live by them to effectively teach life lessons to others.

Being "raised right" doesn't mean you don't drink, party, and smoke.

Being "raised right" is how you treat people, your manners, and respect.

Let Your Character Guide You

There are only two kinds of coaches and administrators: those who have been fired and those who will be. I've been both! In these roles, you need thick skin.

Trying to do the right thing and move forward will inevitably make you a few enemies. The longer you stay, especially beyond five years, the more likely it is that critics will outnumber supporters. Change is necessary, but sometimes it's best for someone new to take the helm.

Take heart, there's always another place that needs your leadership.

If nobody hates you, you're doing something wrong.

Exemplify Positive Leadership

When mentoring a young educator, I spend a lot of time upfront emphasizing confidence and setting clear expectations. To lead others, whether it's a young teacher or a group of students, you must model positivity and a strong, focused attitude.

Those who've worked with me will tell you that my leadership style was grounded in a creed that I hold dear. It reflects my educational philosophy and serves as the foundation of my leadership approach.

Be strong when you are weak

Be brave when you are scared

Be humble when you are victorious

Be badass every day

It is not about being better than someone else

It is about being better than you were the day before.

Be a Decision Maker

As an educational leader, you will face countless opportunities to make decisions that affect your program's success and direction. You must prioritize wisely and consider how each decision impacts both individuals and the group.

Fairness and consistency are essential. Always keep your goals and objectives in mind, and ensure your decisions align with the overall vision of your program.

Success becomes possible when those you lead trust and respect your leadership.

Decisions, not conditions, determine what a man is.

Decision-Making Process

A decision is a conclusion or resolution reached after thoughtful consideration. As an educational leader, you are called upon to make dozens of decisions daily. There are a few important things to remember when doing so. First, never make a decision out of anger, it usually leads to more problems. Strive to make informed decisions, which means gathering all the facts and listening to all sides of the issue.

Second, consider the effects on staff, students, and program participants. Third, set aside personal emotions or biases. This may be the hardest part, especially when you have a vested interest in the situation or the person involved. Later, during the review or evaluation process, you may second-guess yourself, but if your decision was made in the best interest of all parties, you can stand by it with confidence.

Just because a decision hurt does not mean that it was the wrong decision.

Difficulties Provide You an Opportunity to Lead

This lesson says it all. I have led young men and women into the "battle" of competition thousands of times. If you're one of them reading this, you know without a doubt that I stood beside you until the end. I was there in the most difficult situations, we were in it together, and I never blinked.

No matter the outcome, we always took a knee together and gave thanks for the opportunity. I recall a game against the #2 team in the state. They were better than us on paper, but our players were brave and committed. After we lost, we drove to the local emergency room to pick up seven injured players. Thankfully, none of them were seriously hurt. I asked their parents if they could ride the bus back with the team, and they graciously agreed.

I sent an assistant coach to gather the team in the parking lot. Then, with the parents and the injured players, we walked out to meet them. At my request, all 50+ of us took a knee. I told them how proud I was to be their coach and praised their courageous effort that night. We prayed for the injured and said the Lord's Prayer together, out loud, with sincerity and strength.

We boarded the bus and headed home. My players and coaches never knew, but for the next 30 minutes, tears streamed down my face. I gave God the glory for my strength and humility. That team was special. Two years later, many of those same players lifted a championship trophy.

Difficulties show what men are.

-Epictetus

Take a Deep Breath

This simple technique has served me well countless times. I've often written about the importance of taking a deep breath before or during stressful situations. That pause gives you a moment to gather your thoughts and calm your emotions.

As a professional educator, this is a skill you should practice daily. We often face confrontation and misbehavior. In those moments, take a deep breath, relax, listen, and respond as a calm and assertive leader. A good breathing technique is just as effective outside the classroom, in your personal life.

May you never overlook how powerful it can be to slow down for a moment and take a little time to breathe

-Morgan Harper Nichols

Stay Calm, Collected, and Fair

Let's look at decision-making through the lens of success. As an educator, you'll be faced with many decisions throughout your day. If you're a young administrator, teacher, or coach, you'll encounter unfamiliar situations that require judgment, wisdom, and care.

Use your common sense, experience, and intuition to gather the facts. Don't react emotionally or hastily. Instead, take a breath and consider the consequences of your words and actions. Stay calm, manage your emotions, and make thoughtful decisions that serve the group and respect the individual.

Once you've come to a logical conclusion, take action confidently and positively. A good decision is one that contributes to the growth and success of your program.

Indecision is the thief of opportunity.

-Marcus Tullius Cicero

Excellence Is the Foundation

I've never been called a philosopher. But I do have a passion for organized competitive sports, and I've been fortunate to learn from mentors who helped shape my approach to coaching and teaching.

Through these writings, I'm simply trying to share the ideas and practices that helped me build a meaningful career. At every school I served, success was never an accident. It was built. And it was expected.

Excellence is never an accident; it is always the result of high intention, sincere effort, and intelligent execution.

-Aristotle

Build a Program, Establish a Reputation

Texas high school football is unlike anything else in the country. Coaches and players are held publicly accountable every Saturday or Sunday morning during the season. Local newspapers post the scores prominently, often in large headlines across the front page. Inside the sports section, you'll usually find game summaries and detailed box scores.

No other school program is scrutinized in this way. Coaches and players live under a microscope of constant pressure. I sometimes cringe when I hear exaggerated talk about a football program's importance, but here's a fact: one successful season with a three-round playoff run can generate enough revenue to cover the expenses of all other athletic programs in a school district.

That shouldn't be the financial foundation of a school district, but in some places, it is the reality.

It takes a lot of courage to put yourself out there for the world to see and judge through its harsh and critical lens. It takes even more courage ot do it without hiding any parts of yourself and to be completely unapologetic about it.

-JD Lynn

Stand By Your Standards and Reputation

When people don't understand your expectations and standards, they often accuse you of arrogance or condescension. A good leader leads with both positive actions and convincing words. You can lead a horse to water, but it must choose to drink. Eventually, the horse will either drink or wander off to find another watering hole.

Strong people don't have an attitude. They have standards.

Trust Is Your Biggest Asset

I haven't written much about the importance of trust, but it should be emphasized that no meaningful relationship can exist among staff, team members, or students without it. A school's community, administration, staff, and student body must believe in you as their leader. Your bond is your word. Always mean what you say and say what you mean. If you deviate from that, make sure you have a valid reason. Half the people may support you no matter what, but you can be sure the other half are skeptics.

Trust is one of your biggest assets and essential for leaders to have. If trust is violated, it may be lost forever.

-Dr. Patton.

Accountability

This is a lesson I needed to teach my staff, coaches, teachers, and students. Start by admitting your own faults, no one is perfect. They need to know that even you have someone to answer to. It's important they understand that while you are their leader, everyone makes mistakes. Your job is to ensure they learn from them and don't repeat them. Make them aware of **major mistakes** that could result in disciplinary action or removal from responsibilities. Teach them what accountability means: we all answer to someone, and it's not personal when your own feet are held to the fire. The hope is that everyone learns from their errors and improves their craft.

If you can't be corrected without being offended, you will never grow in your life.

Hard Work, Determination, and Positive Reinforcement

As a longtime teacher and coach, my core principles were hard work, determination, and positive reinforcement. As an assistant coach, I earned the respect of both players and colleagues for being demanding and holding high standards. While I knew perfection was unattainable, I pushed for it every day, in practice and in games.

As an athletic director and head football coach, I was meticulous in preparing plays, practices, and game strategies. I was hard on our coaches and even harder on the players. I once coached a team that lacked fundamental skills in tackling, blocking, and physical contact. Before the next season, I called a friend from my time at Oklahoma State. I explained the issue, and he told me, "You need to toughen them up before the first game." He reminded me of a drill we used at OSU called the **Gauntlet Drill**.

At our first summer coaches' meeting, I introduced the drill and showed them a video from OSU. They were shocked I intended to implement it. I won't go into detail here, but let's just say it tested our players' **intestinal fortitude**. Each player had to face their fear of contact, building both confidence and commitment. For the coaches, it was a chance to see who we could truly count on.

That year, we won several close games. The following year, we won the championship. The Gauntlet Drill became a yearly tradition. Former players even returned to support the team before the season began. The drill wasn't just physically demanding, it was spiritually challenging for every player.

Hard is good. The earlier you can learn to deal with hard, the easier it gets...because hard is coming. Whether we want to shield it from kids now or not, hard is coming.

-Greg Olsen

Nurture Success

Many professional educators lose sight of their purpose over the years. They forget that their primary role is to influence and empower kids to become their best selves. I've held many roles in my long career, some were focused on community service and others on achievement, but I never saw success as anything more than helping kids grow and mature.

If you're a young, success-driven teacher or coach, stay focused on your **purpose**, and everything else will fall into place.

Leadership is not about titles, positions, or flowcharts. It is about one life influencing another.

-John C. Maxwell

Be a Person of Values

There's a significant difference between a person's success and their value. Success is relative to the effort put forth in achieving a goal. Value, on the other hand, is measured by the relationships built along the way. Success eventually fades, but meaningful relationships can last a lifetime.

Try not to become a person of success, but rather try to become a person of value.

-*Albert Einstein*

Emphasize the Importance of Values

As an educational leader, I found it critical to teach and coach respect and values. I was once hired by a suburban school district in Dallas to help turn around a struggling middle school of 1,600 students (grades 6–8). The school's academic performance was below expectations, and discipline was in crisis.

I started mid-year at the request of a desperate superintendent. On my first day, I met with the building's administrators. They were good people overwhelmed by constant discipline issues and teacher negativity. I promised immediate and positive change.

Next, I met with the entire staff, from teachers to custodians, and laid out my vision and expectations. Their initial response was skeptical. The first step was to get students to class on time and keep them there. I had all teachers stand in the hallways during passing periods, greeting students and guiding them to class. When the tardy bell rang, they were to close and lock their doors. Any students left in the halls were rounded up by five administrators and our campus police officer and taken to the cafeteria for processing. Each student received a consequence and their parents were contacted. Within two weeks, **98% of students were on time**.

After several months of observation and conversation, we determined most students lacked proper social skills and self-discipline. That summer, I sent our teachers to Boys Town Training and Conflict Resolution Camp. We implemented the training in the fall.

We also trained teachers to disaggregate test data and focus on weak areas. By the third school year, our scores rated as **Exceeds Expectations**, and we reduced discipline referrals by **90%**. All it took was a commitment to teaching strong values and addressing student needs.

Change is always possible, with determination and effort.

Education without values, as useful as it is, seems rather to make man a more clever devil.

-C.S. Lewis

Build Credibility With the Truth

Truth is the quality of being genuine, accurate, and factual. As a leader, truth is a fundamental building block in establishing credibility with both staff and participants. It's often said that the truth will set you free, I would add that it also opens the door to changing cultural habits. As a professional educator, I emphasized that honesty is the best policy. I taught that truth is essential for developing strong character.

Being truthful also means accepting the consequences of your actions when you're wrong. If more families taught this principle at home, we'd see greater civility and understanding in everyday life.

Be Inspirational

As a professional educator, I believe that you are the most important role model in a child's life. What's a role model? It's someone whose life and character inspire you to imitate and aspire to their qualities. Powerful, right? Kids are often easy to read, if they like you, you'll see it in their smile; if they don't, you'll sense it in their silence or frown.

Sometimes, you'll get mixed signals, and it can be confusing. But if you take pride in your work, make sure to also take pride in the impression you leave on your students. Your influence on their development is far greater than you may ever realize.

Hold your tongue and live your life, for it is in the way that you live that you speak the loudest.

Display Eternal Optimism

This philosophy has guided me in every leadership role I've held, as an administrator, teacher, and coach. It's crucial to approach each day with optimism and hope. Staff and students look to you to set the tone and model a strong work ethic.

I always focused on building confidence and character in our programs. Yes, challenges and setbacks are inevitable and often frustrating. But those emotions should be processed in private, away from others. This is difficult but necessary to preserve a positive atmosphere. Once you've worked through the issue, find your solution, adjust your path, and move forward.

The pessimist
complains about the wind.
The optimist expects
it to change.
The leader adjusts the sails.

Model Your Expectations

As a leader, it's vital to clearly demonstrate the behaviors and values you expect from others. If you want your team to follow, you must first model respect, honesty, trust, and loyalty. People won't fully commit until they know what to expect from you.

Respect is earned.

Honesty is appreciated.

Trust is gained.

Loyalty is returned.

Teach the Attributes of Winning and Losing

One of the most important responsibilities of an administrator, teacher, or coach is helping students grow through both victory and defeat. Their personal development often unfolds right before your eyes. They rely on your guidance, not just when things are going well, but especially during setbacks.

It's not always about winning. Sometimes, it's about learning from mistakes, accepting loss, and staying humble. Show students that hard work and determination prepare them for future opportunities. As the leader, take every chance to teach life lessons.

In life's arena, success and failure dance together, teaching resilience and growth.

Establish a Connection

When working with other people's children, it's crucial they sense your sincerity and feel connected to your message. They need to believe in you before they can receive instruction from you. This bond of trust must be built for real success to occur.

You are important and you matter.

Your voice matters.

Your life matters.

Your feelings matter.

Your story matters.

Always.

Be Insightful

This quality is often overlooked. All your life experiences, knowledge, and awareness offer valuable insights that help you anticipate challenges and respond thoughtfully. This ability has served me well in striving to be the best person and professional I can be.

You have three eyes.
Two to look.
One to see.

Perception Influences Judgment

Stay open-minded when addressing difficult or complex issues, but don't dismiss your instincts. Often, things are just as they appear. The deeper question is how you approach redemption. Can you look beyond someone's misstep to help them grow from the consequences?

Every challenge can be a learning experience. Your final decision may be tough, but when made with integrity, it will usually be respected.

Leadership is about making others better as a result of your presence and making sure that impact lasts in your absence.

Empower Members of Your Organization

I learned early on that a strong organization depends on each member knowing their contributions matter. When people are empowered to participate in decisions, they begin to take ownership.

Not everyone seeks responsibility, but you can guide and encourage them to become engaged. Over time, the team transforms into a united, high-performing group. It's truly a beautiful thing to witness.

The most common way people give up their power is by thinking they don't have any.

-Alice Walker

Give Credit Where Credit Is Due

I've never sought the spotlight. My leadership style has always focused on shared objectives and recognizing the team. Without the dedication of staff and support personnel, our successes wouldn't have been possible.

I used to tell star athletes, "You wouldn't be here without the blockers who protect you." Their acknowledgment of the team fostered a mindset of "we" instead of "me." People are more likely to invest in progress when they feel ownership in the process.

True service lies in helping people thrive without seeking ownership or gratitude.

-Lao Tzu

Recognize the Needs of Others

Everyone needs recognition and appreciation now and then, though not everyone wants attention. As a leader, you must be sensitive to individual needs.

Create a welcoming environment where people feel secure and trusted. Encourage participation and engagement while addressing dissatisfaction with care. A great leader helps people feel both seen and heard.

Don't be the reason someone feels insecure.

Be the reason someone feels seen, heard, and supported by the whole universe.

Cultivate the Seed

If you're an educator, you must understand that all students can learn, just not all at the same pace or in the same way. Your responsibility is to identify and apply effective strategies to plant the seeds of knowledge and nurture their growth.

The tiny seed knew that in order to grow, it needed to be dropped in dirt, covered in darkness, and struggle to reach the light.

Choose Your Words Carefully

Be aware, your words have an immediate impact. Effective communication starts with your mindset. Don't respond on an emotional whim. Instead, pause. Give yourself 10–15 seconds to calm down by taking a deep breath and exhaling. As a leader, your words can significantly influence outcomes and resolutions. Be intentional, say what you mean, and mean what you say.

The tongue has no bones. But it is strong enough to break a heart. So be careful with your words.

Discipline Management

When developing a program, discipline can be defined as the ability to behave and work in a controlled and consistent way by following specific rules or standards. It is not simply obedience to avoid punishment. Instead, discipline involves adopting and applying intentional standards to reach meaningful objectives. Discipline is a choice. When implementing cultural change, a leader must establish clear standards, model the expected behavior, and hold staff and participants accountable.

Discipline is about making choice after choice that's aligned with our intentions.

In any moment, we can make a choice that supports an intention; or we can make a choice that supports an old habit, a lack of intention or a fear.

-Chetna Mehta

Address Student Behavior

As an educational leader, I was always concerned when professionals didn't recognize the importance of classroom management and setting expectations. I once believed this was a challenge unique to new teachers or coaches. However, I've seen many experienced educators who also struggle in this area. It's like teaching in the dark, students notice, take advantage, and often show disrespect.

If you're a young educator struggling with classroom management, don't worry. There are mentor teachers and coaches on every campus. All you have to do is ask one for help or advice, most are more than willing to share what works for them.

Veteran teachers or coaches who consistently fail in this area may require a different approach. As the leader, you might need to implement a growth plan and observe their performance more frequently. They must either improve or consider other options.

We can easily forgive a child who is afraid of the dark; the real tragedy of life is when men are afraid of the light.

-Plato

Be Tough, Not Popular

Throughout my career, I've worked with tens of thousands of teenagers. With most of them, I emphasized the importance of looking inward for strength, growth, and purpose. Many were exploring their identities and futures, and I felt a strong responsibility to highlight the abundance of opportunity in this country.

I wasn't speaking about equality; I was emphasizing opportunity. My message was always honest and grounded in truth: every choice carries consequences. While each of us has the freedom to choose, none of us are free from the outcomes those choices bring.

Many of the programs I created and led included daily activities focused on choices and consequences. That's one of the great benefits of extracurricular involvement; it teaches life skills that last far beyond the classroom.

Accept People for Who They Are

This is a critical lesson for young coaches and teachers. Yes, you must have high expectations, consistent rules, and clear team or class goals. These are fundamental to effective discipline management.

But within that structure, it's essential to recognize that each student or athlete is a unique individual, shaped by their environment and personality. Your intuition and understanding are vital when dealing with challenges and negative behaviors.

Your perception matters, don't try to force a square peg into a round hole. Maintain your standards, but never lose sight of the relationships you build. They are just as important as the discipline you uphold.

The Truth: Documentation Is Imperative

I served as a school administrator for 15 years of my career. Many of you might be surprised by the number of different versions of "the truth" I've heard over the years. In many cases, I already knew the real story, but I was always curious to hear and observe facts from the other side of an issue. My responsibility was to enforce school district policies and procedures, or uphold team rules and expectations set by coaches and the athletic department.

So many incidents and conflicting accounts were presented to me that I couldn't begin to recount them all!

Here's a widely accepted definition of truth: *the quality of being true, genuine, actual, or factual.*

If you're a young teacher or coach, I cannot stress enough the importance of **documentation**. This refers to your written record of facts, documenting behavior, attitudes, or inappropriate language. Whether you're in the classroom, on the field, or on the court, **this is your domain**. Your rules and expectations matter, and your ability to hold participants accountable is essential. But you'll be at a disadvantage if you rely solely on your word.

This also applies to coaches during practices and games. Keep a simple record of problematic students or incidents, it only takes a moment to note the date, time, and behavior. One last and crucial step: contact the parent as soon as possible with a phone call or email. Often, parents can help address their child's behavior. But be aware, sometimes, the parent may be part of the problem.

In closing, **the truth usually supports your position**, as long as you give it a little attention and preparation. As an administrator, I always tried to support my teachers and coaches. There were times when this was difficult. In such cases, I turned the situation into a learning experience for both of us, hoping to help them grow stronger in our shared profession.

Learn to deal with people for who they are, not who you want them to be.

Life gets a lot easier when you stop expecting apple juice from an orange.

Consistent Discipline Matters

One of my least favorite responsibilities as an assistant principal was handling student discipline. My first job in this role was especially challenging, but I understood that I had been hired to help improve campus-wide behavior issues. Over a few years, we successfully developed and maintained a strong discipline management program.

I was responsible for students with last names from F to P, about 700 kids. Of those, I spent the majority of my time addressing the misbehavior of around 50. I left that position after three years, worn out from chasing the same students day after day. It just wasn't fun anymore, and I rarely had the chance to interact with the well-behaved kids. So, I returned to coaching and teaching, my first passion.

About ten years later, I was giving a ride home to one of our players after practice. We stopped at a 7-Eleven so he could grab a snack, as his mother was working late. While paying at the counter, the player pointed out that a woman and her kids were following me through the store and were now waiting outside. He asked if I knew them. I told him I didn't think so.

As we exited, the woman grabbed my sleeve and asked if I recognized her. I asked if I was supposed to. She called me *Coach Kelly* and reminded me of a discipline referral that had landed her in my office many years ago. I remembered her once she refreshed my memory.

She told me that our encounter had *literally changed the course of her life*. I had counseled her about her potential, scolded her for lashing out at a teacher, and then walked her back to that classroom where she publicly apologized in front of her peers. The teacher accepted her apology graciously and invited her to return to her seat.

The woman thanked me for how I handled that situation. She then introduced me to her children and told me she had graduated with honors, gone on to study engineering at Texas A&M, and was now enjoying a successful career as an engineer. I congratulated her, shook her hand and her kids' hands, and went on my way.

As I dropped the player off at his home, he told me that the experience with the woman and her family was "pretty neat," a moment he said he wouldn't soon forget.

When you fill the role of a leader, you aren't a monarch and placed above others; you are a servant responsible for influencing, mentoring, and developing those you lead!

-Dr. Patton

Be Tough, Not Popular

I've had the privilege of working with tens of thousands of teenagers during my career. I made it a point to help most of them look inward, toward their own strength, growth, and passion. Many were exploring, testing boundaries, and thinking about their futures. I always felt a deep responsibility to emphasize the abundance of opportunities available in America.

We live in a country where the right to choose is protected. I wasn't necessarily talking about equality, I was talking about **opportunity**. It was important that my message be **honest and truthful**. I wanted them to understand that with every choice comes a consequence. Though we are free to choose, we are not free from the consequences of those choices.

Most of the programs I developed and supervised included daily lessons on choices and consequences. This is one of the greatest benefits of extracurricular school activities.

Accept People for Who They Are

This is a crucial lesson for young teachers and coaches. You should maintain high expectations, clear rules, and team goals. These are essential for effective discipline and classroom management. But within this structure, you must also recognize that every student or athlete is an individual, with unique personalities, backgrounds, and environmental challenges.

Your ability to be understanding, intuitive, and perceptive is key when addressing problems and negative behavior. You can't fit a square peg into a round hole. Don't sacrifice your team's integrity, but always value the relationships you build with your students and athletes.

Be Judicial With the Truth

If you're still in the classroom or on the sidelines coaching, know this: not everyone can handle your version of the truth. A true professional learns to share just enough to keep the student or athlete motivated, and the parent supportive.

Your full evaluation and strategy should be carefully considered, and often kept behind closed doors. The goal should always be to promote growth through positive reinforcement and encouragement. That's usually where true progress begins.

Being an honest and truthful person does not mean that you will tell everyone everything. You need to protect your truth, your story, and your emotions in this cruel, judgmental, and fake world.

- Rahul Kaushik

Display Your Humanity as the Leader

Throughout my career as an agent of change, I've learned much from the experience. Ironically, I'm not a huge fan of change in my personal life. Life is unpredictable, and the idea of control is an illusion.

You find a partner and start building a life, but things happen. Sometimes it lasts, other times it doesn't. You raise children, they grow up, things get complicated, and eventually, they go out into the world. At that point, all you can do is be there for them as they build their own lives.

Careers rise and fall, and you adapt to changing circumstances. Life's factors shape us all. What matters is how we emotionally respond to change. Laugh at the funny moments, smile at the joys, cry through the losses, love your close ones deeply, and celebrate your victories.

Above all else, give God the glory and honor for blessing your life and guiding your spirit.

There is no manual for navigating through this life. There's a constant mix of joys, disappointments, laughter, love, and loss. The hardest of which is the gradual learning that comes after sudden changes.

-Jay Long

Success Is Earned Through Commitment

Let this be a message to those who hear my reflections: Many people support the idea of giving a ribbon or trophy to every participant. But this mindset can undermine the true spirit of competition.

Success is directly tied to a person's work ethic, expectations, and commitment to excellence. Those who make a genuine effort to improve themselves and their circumstances deserve recognition. Those who do not should still be encouraged, but reminded that effort is essential if they want to be acknowledged.

We live in the greatest country in the world when it comes to opportunity. But opportunity should not simply be handed out, it should be earned.

Most people don't want to be part of the process; they just want to be part of the outcome. But the process is where you figure out who's worth being part of the outcome.

-Scottie Pippen

Motivation and Leadership

I'll admit, as the leader of my team or organization, I always aimed to be the calm before the storm. But my players and students knew without a doubt that I was in it to win it, right alongside them.

There are plenty out there who remember my pregame or halftime speeches. In those moments, I'm sure someone was holding my halo, because I never held back. My fire, passion, and emotion were that of a warrior, going into battle beside each one of them.

Before stepping into the arena, we always prayed for guidance and protection. And once the moment had passed, I'd find my halo and place it back where it belonged.

Many who went through it with me still hold a vivid memory of those moments.

Most times I will tell you
"I am the calm before the storm",
But sometimes I will say
"here, hold my halo
I'm going in."
-L.L.

Share Your Light and Opportunity

Many students and staff members needed my emotional strength and attention over the years. When your spiritual light is burning and you're truly listening, you'll notice those around you whose spirits need a boost. You don't have to be nosy or intrusive to brighten someone's day or help them through a tough situation.

One situation comes to mind immediately. One night, I received a phone call from a former player, an incredible athlete and even better person, who was a valued part of our program. He told me about a talented player who had recently moved into our district and needed my help. The young man had dropped out of school the previous spring. His father had passed away suddenly during Christmas break, and the loss devastated him. He withdrew from school and fell into a deep emotional hole.

I told my former player to bring him up to the school the next morning. I wouldn't be there, but I'd notify the counselor and my secretary that he was coming, and we would work with him. I followed through, gave the heads-up, and left for my meeting. When I returned, my secretary informed me that the new student had arrived and was in the counselor's office. I dropped off my things and went straight there.

As I entered, the counselor was just leaving. I asked about the new student, and he said he'd already walked him to class. When I asked why he enrolled him without my approval, the counselor responded, "Have you seen this kid?" I admitted I hadn't but mentioned I'd heard he was a good athlete. The counselor looked me squarely in the eye and said, "You need to go meet him. Then you'll understand."

I headed to the portable classroom, knocked on the door, and the teacher answered. I apologized for the interruption and asked to speak with the student. She called him to the door and resumed teaching. I leaned against the railing, waiting. When the door opened, this *man* bent down to step through it. Standing 6'9" and weighing 290 lbs, he was one of the largest young men I'd ever seen. I introduced myself and reached out to shake his hand, which completely engulfed mine. I instantly understood the counselor's urgency.

In just a few minutes of conversation, I could tell he was intelligent, well-spoken, and respectful. I later learned his grades had been excellent before he dropped out. For 18 months, I supported him and pushed him to catch up. He did. Not only did he succeed academically, but he also became an All-District and All-City football player who earned the opportunity to compete at the next level. I loved that kid. He became a great teammate and a bright light in our program.

One of the most important things you can do on this earth is to let people know they are not alone.

-Shannon L. Alder

251

Hearts and Souls

Eddie Robinson, one of the winningest college football coaches in history, produced more NFL prospects than many major universities. A legend in his own right, he described leadership as a fight for the heart and soul of the young men in his care. He believed in creating a bond built on trust and inspiration to help them believe that anything was possible. His philosophy centered on instilling confidence, character, commitment, and genuine concern into each athlete's heart and soul.

Leadership, like coaching, is fighting for the hearts and souls of men and getting them to believe in you.

-Eddie Robinson

Bravery and Preparation

How do you accomplish the impossible as a leader? Many of you will face extremely difficult situations in your careers. When preparing students or athletes for those challenges, remember: "impossible" is a mindset.

Teach your students to look beyond apparent disadvantages. Help them focus on preparation, hard work, and determination. Highlight their strengths and foster mental toughness. Remind them that mistake-free execution is within their grasp. They must believe in their own capability. Never let the talent or reputation of the opponent become the focus. Your positivity, confidence, and emotional strength will carry over to them. They will feel it.

The bravest are surely those who have the clearest vision of what is before them, glory and danger alike, and yet notwithstanding, go out to meet it.

-Thucydides

Establish a Good Work Ethic

I have to admit, I always hated practice. As a player, coach, and head coach, those hours spent fine-tuning alignments, timing, and movements were tough. But I was determined: no opponent would ever outwork or out-prepare us. It takes incredible discipline and commitment to build that kind of work ethic. But the reward isn't just in winning. It's in the deep satisfaction of knowing the effort was worth it. Practice doesn't make you perfect, but it makes you *believe* that you can be.

You don't show up on game day and expect to be great. Greatness happens in practice. You have to expect things of yourself before you can do them.

-Michael Jordan

Encourage Lifetime Progress

I want to celebrate all those I've influenced over the past 40 years who rose above their circumstances and built a better life for themselves and their families. I'm incredibly proud and inspired by your achievements.

I know many of you grew up in loving, secure environments. But I also know you dreamed of a future that went beyond what you had. You wanted more, and you made it happen. Today, I see the photos and celebrations you share of your children and grandchildren succeeding. It's a testament to your resilience and drive.

You deserve to be commended.

Those who can see beyond the shadows and lies of their culture will never be understood, let alone believed, by the masses.

-Plato

Expand Your Comfort Zone

This is a lesson we can all benefit from. Like many things in life, change is inevitable. Each of us has boundaries that define our comfort zone, but most growth and progress occur beyond those limits. A great leader learns to expand their comfort zone and face change head-on. This is how hope grows and matures. The ability to assess priorities, think creatively, consider alternative solutions, and evaluate compromises helps expand a leader's capacity. It's important to remain understanding and flexible while staying focused and assertive.

Very few things of growth happen inside the comfort zone.

Don't Be Complacent or Dismissive

This message serves as a warning to all young administrators, teachers, and coaches who are making a difference. I admire and respect you deeply, and I pray for you daily. A good educator understands that staff, parents, and students make mistakes, and most will learn from them over time. However, acts of disrespect, dishonesty, and disloyalty are never acceptable. If you become complacent or dismissive of such behavior, it will only create more problems and hinder progress. As an educator, learn to recognize the difference and respond accordingly.

Mistakes happen and mistakes can be forgiven, but lies and disloyalty are a deliberate act of betrayal...

Encourage Self-Perception

I learned this lesson early in my career. As a professional educator, you are a role model for those you serve. Some students already have strong personalities and defined character. Others are still finding their way, and you may play a significant role in their development. Knowing this, you should help them discover what motivates and inspires them. Encourage them to pursue their passions and interests. In doing so, you are nurturing their self-perception and personal growth.

Be a Facilitator

I believe Bruce Lee was right when he said: a good teacher teaches facts, not their own interpretation or personal impressions. A student's mind is still developing and highly impressionable. Personal opinions and biases should be left to the parents or guardians. Teachers take on a variety of important roles in the lives of their students. This should be considered carefully when planning, preparing, and implementing daily lessons. Keep your teaching professionally objective, and leave personal agendas outside the classroom.

A teacher is never a giver of truth: he is a guide, a pioneer to the truth that each student must find for himself.

-Bruce Lee

Students Are a Product of Their Environment

As an educator and administrator, this is one of the most important lessons I've learned. Some children's behaviors are directly modeled after the adults in their lives. There have been times during conferences with parents when I realized that the parent's behavior was even more troubling than the child's. Trusting my instincts helped me find ways to guide these children toward positive, healthy behaviors and a greater sense of normalcy.

Be Influential in Their Lives

To all the young men I've had the honor of influencing, my hope was always to help you become the best son, father, and grandfather you could be. I aimed to instill confidence, character, commitment, and compassion. Many of you are now navigating adulthood, and I hope your integrity and passion for life shine through and inspire your own sons.

The greatness of a man is not in how much wealth he acquires, but in his integrity and his ability to affect those around him positively.

— Bob Marley

Be a Positive Father Figure

While mothers are undoubtedly the rock of the family, the father's role cannot be overstated. This is why I strongly support the importance of two-parent households. The bond between father and son is powerful and vital. As a former coach, I know firsthand how often male coaches become father figures in single-parent homes. Though I never had sons of my own, only daughters, I was blessed with thousands of "sons" through coaching. Many of you know who you are and how much you mean to me.

When you teach your son, you teach your son's son.

Positive Administrative Leadership Is Essential

As someone who has built and led many programs, I learned early on that the success of any program largely depends on the support of administration and the school board. Since administrators manage the day-to-day operations of a school district, their backing is crucial. However, their job security is often tied to the politics of the school board. That's why maintaining strong, respectful relationships with your administration is essential. When the climate changes or negativity arises, trust your instincts. Be realistic, seek the next opportunity, and continue to share your expertise, there is always a door waiting for you to walk through it.

Either they like you or they don't. Never try to convince somebody of our worth. If a person doesn't appreciate you, they don't deserve you. Respect yourself and be with people who truly value you.

Evade Distractions

I speak about this often because it's such a common issue. Obstacles and distractions can derail progress. A distraction is anything that prevents someone from fully focusing on the task at hand. As a young teacher or coach, you must learn how to reduce or manage them. Several strategies can help:

- Continue teaching or coaching without acknowledging the distraction. This may seem passive but often proves effective by denying the attention-seeker the spotlight.

- Move the disruptive student closer to the door as a subtle warning, the message is clear: their behavior will be removed if it doesn't improve.

- In more severe cases, remove the individual from the environment and resume your lesson.

- Alternatively, redirect them with another activity to help refocus their energy before resorting to removal.

These methods also worked with my athletes. Do everything in your power to reduce distractions and maintain focus and momentum.

People who say it cannot be done should not interrupt those who are doing it.

-George B. Shaw

Evaluation Is the Gateway to Success

I suppose I'm writing this in retrospect. This is a lesson I learned over the course of 40 years. Let's begin with losses and failures. When you've been in this business as long as I have, you will inevitably face your share of setbacks. It's fair to say that I felt each one deeply, both personally and professionally. However, I learned to gather my strength and rely on my faith to lead my team forward.

Remember, you are the leader, and your team will follow your example. Manage your emotions, adopt a positive attitude, and tackle mistakes head-on to make progress.

Now, let's talk about wins and successes, because celebrating achievements is never difficult. Enjoy and savor those moments as they happen, but then set them aside and evaluate. There is always room for improvement and growth. You should continuously assess performance and stay committed to your plan. Get your staff, parents, and students back into the routine with repetition and focus. Put your ego aside, there's always another challenge just around the corner.

"Never let success go to your head,
and never
let failures go to your heart."

Daily Review and Reflection

As an educational leader for most of my career, I quickly learned the importance of daily evaluation and adjustment. You can make plans and set objectives, but unexpected situations arise every day. Naturally, these require you to make necessary adjustments and detours. This is not to discourage thorough preparation, but to emphasize the importance of daily review. Before moving forward each day, ask yourself reflective questions to guide your decisions.

Leadership Journal Prompts

What are you most afraid of from the previous day?	*How did I stumble as a leader yesterday?*
What am I thankful for right now?	*If I lived yesterday over again, what would I do differently?*

Leadership

To me, a leader is someone who inspires passion and motivation in others. A leader has a vision and a clear path to achieving it. A leader ensures their team has the support and tools needed to succeed.

Are you a leader? I knew from the young age of 15 that I possessed leadership qualities. By my junior year in high school, I realized my growing skills allowed me to positively influence my classmates and teammates. I served on the junior board of directors for the only bank in town, ranked in the top 10 of my class, was a member of the National Honor Society, defensive captain and play caller for our varsity football team, president of the Fellowship of Christian Athletes, and the recognized leader of my church youth group.

Through these roles, I gained valuable experience and insight in working with people. At 20, I landed my first coaching job as a graduate assistant and dormitory director at Oklahoma State University. I spent four years as an assistant coach and teacher at the high school level. By age 26, I became the youngest athletic director and head football coach in Texas at a 4A/5A school, the two largest classifications in the state.

Over the next 26 years, the Lord blessed me with many opportunities to lead and positively transform the cultures of thousands of students and athletes. In the beginning, my leadership skills were raw and unrefined. But as my career advanced, my philosophy and expectations matured into a true passion.

A leader is one who knows the way, goes the way and shows the way.

PARTICIPANT DEVELOPMENT

Welcome the Journey

Over the past 40 years, my professional journey has provided me with many beginnings and endings. Most of these stops were in places that needed my skills as an agent of change and progress. I have already discussed the principles and objectives required to initiate such changes. I want you to know that each of these opportunities presented different scenarios and circumstances. Still, I was able to rely on similar action plans and the same will and determination.

That said, I began each job with reservations, concerns, and insecurities. I encourage you to trust your inner voice and spirit to move forward. When the end comes, move on without regret, you were there for a reason and with a purpose. Every place I left was in a better situation than when I arrived. One thing I knew for sure: the kids and the community had learned enough to sustain their progress and continue moving forward. It can be a sad time, but you carry great memories and lasting friendships with you.

Beginnings are usually scary and endings are usually sad, but it's everything in between that makes it all worth living.

-Bob Marley

Praise, Positive Reinforcement, and Encouragement

This is how you begin to create cultural change within a program. Praise, positive reinforcement, encouragement, concern, and a direct interest in both personal and program growth are all critical. As the leader, you must find ways to include your administration, community, and teaching staff. Winning early and becoming competitive quickly certainly helps, but your positive attitude and salesmanship play an essential role in winning over any doubters. When you combine all of these efforts, you will see progress. You just have to believe!

Be aware of what others are doing, applaud their efforts, acknowledge their successes, and encourage them in their pursuits. When we all help one another, everybody wins.

Build Participant Leadership Skills

Some of my earlier comments have addressed leadership and sportsmanship. If you are a young teacher or coach, understand that the success of your group does not rest solely on your leadership. It often depends on certain group members who step up and lead through adversity. Your ability to recognize, encourage, and utilize these young leaders is essential to the success of the group.

Bad teams, no one leads.

Average teams, caches lead.

But elite teams, players lead.

-P. J. Fleck

Team-Building Attributes

When leading educational programs, remember that talent levels vary. Therefore, success often depends on other factors. It is crucial to emphasize, encourage, and teach personal attributes that help build a stronger group or team. These attributes require no natural talent but significantly contribute to group achievement.

10 things that require zero talent:

1. *Being on time*

2. *Making an effort*

3. *Being high energy*

4. *Having a positive attitude*

5. *Being passionate*

6. *Using good body language*

7. *Being teachable*

8. *Doing a little extra*

9. *Being prepared*

10. *Having a strong work ethic*

Encourage Teamwork and Concern

A reward is something given in return for a good deed, a service rendered, or merit earned through hard work, determination, and positive thinking. As a young teacher or coach, help your participants visualize the reward earned by their efforts. While winning is certainly part of success, the greatest rewards come from giving of yourself, bettering the lives of others, being part of something greater, and making a meaningful difference.

As a coach, remember: many of the most important lessons in coaching have little to do with winning and everything to do with how we handle defeat. Accomplishing the seemingly impossible is more than a reward, it's a lifetime achievement.

The most rewarding things you do in life are often the
ones that look like they cannot be done.

Hold Participants to a Higher Standard

As a young teacher or coach, understand that you are a significant influence in your students' lives. You set the goals, objectives, and standards for learning and growth. Set the bar high and respectable, then hold your students to it. Let your actions and expectations be driven by genuine concern and commitment. The ultimate goals are growth, maturity, and progress.

Being coached hard is not abuse. Being held to high standards for your own growth and development is not abuse. Loving your athletes enough to not let them settle is not abuse. Improvement and success don't come on the back of a unicorn galloping over a rainbow.

Emphasize Willpower

When I speak of a person's "will," I refer to willpower, the ability to resist short-term temptation in pursuit of long-term goals. Sometimes it's called determination or self-control. Willpower is what drives a person to make sacrifices for long-term success. As an educational leader, you'll need a strong will to overcome negative circumstances and obstacles. I once coached a 190-pound Indonesian shot putter. He began in 10th grade with a 38' shot put and a 110' discus throw. Two years later, he led the North Texas region with a 59' shot put and a 185' discus throw. These achievements earned him a full college scholarship and eventually a nursing degree. His accomplishments were the result of hard work, determination, and a powerful will. Seventeen years later, I still hold the utmost admiration and respect for him. I've only known one person with a stronger will, and that's me.

It's hard to beat a person who never gives up.

- *Babe Ruth*

Teach Courageousness

Courage is the mental or moral strength to persevere, to withstand fear, danger, or difficulty. It's the internal fortitude to face adversity and still perform. As a teacher or coach, I've led many young men and women into the lion's den of academic and athletic challenges. The outcomes have been mixed, but the lessons were lasting.

Success wasn't always about gaining or winning. It was about building strength, confidence, and character. These are the qualities they carry into their lives, qualities that help them achieve real success. Sometimes, this leads to accomplishments no one thought possible.

Courage is not a man with a gun in his hand. It's knowing you're licked before you begin, but you begin anyway, and you see it through no matter what. You rarely win, but sometimes you do.

-    *Harper Lee*

Cultural Change, Teach Social Skills

If you work with other people's children, you must remember this lesson: you will be confronted with a variety of problems and situations that demand your understanding. I'm not saying to reward disobedience or inappropriate behavior, discipline is a necessary element in raising expectations. But a good educator cannot ignore a lack of social skills, special needs, foster care situations, multiple stepparents, single-parent families, and more. I could go on and on about the possible disadvantages facing students and athletes.

I once served as an assistant principal on a campus of 1,600 sixth, seventh, and eighth graders. I took the job in December at the request of a superintendent, who was a good friend, and it was his most troubled campus. At my first administrative meeting, the other four campus administrators brought their discipline referral charts and piles of unprocessed referrals. In that first semester, there had been 93 fights and over 100 outstanding referrals. We cleared the backlog and put students on notice about their behavior and the importance of getting to class on time. I addressed this the old-fashioned way, with a bullhorn and consistent reinforcement.

After realizing that 40% of our students lived in the Barbara Jordan Housing Project in Dallas, we understood that many of them lacked social skills and structure. So, we sent part of our teaching staff to Lincoln, Nebraska, that summer to learn the elements of the Boys Town Training program for teaching social skills. The other half attended conflict resolution training at SMU. The next year, we launched a school-wide training program for students called "Increase the Peace." At first, it was met with resistance, but we moved forward anyway. Two years later, fights were reduced to just one, and discipline referrals had dropped by 90%. It can be done, if you're willing to be empathetic in your approach!

Nothing is more important than empathy for another human being's suffering. Nothing. Not career, not wealth, not intelligence, certainly not status. We have to feel for one another if we're going to survive with dignity.

- Audrey Hepburn

Teach Accountability

This lesson is about accepting responsibility for your own actions and stopping the blame game. Don't blame the teacher or coach for your circumstances. Every professional educator sets behavioral rules and expectations for the students and athletes they influence. If you're one of them, you have a decision to make: you can acknowledge the expectations and work hard to be the best you can be, or you can choose to walk away and accept the consequences.

There are always a few who stay and test the teacher or coach's resolve, but they will eventually need to decide what is best for themselves. As a professional, I always tried to welcome and serve everyone, but I also recognized that participation is a privilege, not a right. I would work with you and help provide structure and discipline, but I would never make the decision to conform for you. Know this: your decision isn't about whether I like you, it's about the growth, development, and success of the group. Your decision must reflect whether you want to be a productive member of that group.

Stop saying that Coach doesn't like you.

Coaches don't like:

1. *A lack of effort*
2. *Showing up late for practice*
3. *Talking when they are talking*
4. *Failing grade check*
5. *Not following instructions*
6. *Being asked to put you in the game*
7. *Poor sportsmanship*
8. *Lack of skill development*
9. *Talking back*
10. *Talking trash about teammateS*

Teach and Exemplify Sportsmanship

Good sportsmanship means being able to win without gloating, respecting your opponents, and losing with grace. Key qualities of sportsmanship include:

1. **Being supportive**. Don't take your disappointment out on teammates.

2. **Having a positive attitude**

3. **Showing respect**

4. **Being willing to learn**

5. **Practicing self-control**

Fairness, integrity, responsibility, and respect are the four pillars of sportsmanship. As an athletic director, I made good sportsmanship a non-negotiable expectation, and a requirement, for continued participation in our programs.

Encourage Them to Build Upon Their Dreams

When you lead a program, you become the bridge between dreams and possibilities. Never offer guarantees, but always provide expectation, knowledge, and hope. And yes, if it sounds like you're becoming a kind of salesperson, that's because you are. You'll need to be a master motivator, a public relations expert, an effective disciplinarian, and an open-minded problem solver. But above all, you will be the purveyor of dreams for your staff, students, and athletes.

A dream is what the heart
whispers to the silence of your mind.

Dance With the One That Brought You

This lesson is about tolerance and acceptance. As a leader, you must teach students and athletes to recognize and embrace their differences. My career placed me in many new environments filled with diverse personalities and challenges. It's important to welcome those differences, respect all opinions, and acknowledge everyone's contributions. However, I never let any of that distract me from the goal. I kept moving forward, implementing strategies to create a more positive and competitive culture. You must stay focused.

We can't always choose the music life plays for us, but we can choose how we dance to it.

Teach Them How to Grow From Losing

Serena Williams is a gracious example of both competitiveness and sportsmanship. She often speaks about learning from her losses. Those who know me understand my drive and determination to win, but I always emphasized the value of learning from mistakes. Losing can become a habit if you let it. To reverse that, you must recognize and identify what went wrong, and then take deliberate action to ensure those mistakes don't happen again. I call this the *learning effect*.

I don't like to lose at anything… yet I've grown most not from victories, but setbacks. If winning is god's reward, then losing is how he teaches us.

- *Serena Williams*

Seize the Opportunity to Teach Them About Life

Here's the thing about being a successful administrator, teacher, or coach: you have the opportunity to help students understand how life responds to both adversity and triumph. Student growth and maturity often unfold right before your eyes. They depend on your guidance.

It's not always about success and winning. Many times, it's about learning from defeat and disappointment. Teach them to learn from their mistakes, and to be humble when they win. Show them that hard work and determination prepare them for the next challenge. As their leader, you must seize every opportunity to teach them about life.

In life's arena, Success and Failure dance together, teaching resilience and growth.

PROFESSIONAL EXPECTATIONS

Passionate About Education

I've always had a passion for coaching and teaching. From the beginning of my long career, I knew God had given me the ability to make a positive and lasting impact on the lives of my students and athletes. I've watched many of them grow into outstanding professionals, parents, and community leaders. It's a great privilege to be part of that process!

What you leave behind is not what is engraved in stone monuments, but what is woven into the lives of others.

-Pericles

Believe in Your Destiny

Let me be clear about destiny: when you set out to change a program's culture, stay positive and move forward with your goals and expectations. You'll face adversity, roadblocks, and obstacles along the way, but you're the leader. Positive reinforcement and your glowing energy will lead to change. Stay the course and keep moving forward. Progress will come if you are patient.

Everything will work out in the end. You don't need to know how. You just have to trust that it will. Never let a bad situation bring out the worst in you.

Be strong and choose to be positive

Stand for Who You Are

I love this lesson. Toward the end of my career, I accepted a position as a defensive coordinator and taught Government and Economics. It was a good job with an amazing staff and great kids. I initially planned to stay a year or two before moving on, but the contract was excellent, and I grew to love the community. I ended up staying four years until health issues finally forced me into retirement.

When I turned in my resignation, I had an exit interview with the Head Coach and Athletic Coordinator, a good man and friend whom I deeply respected. The last thing he said to me was:

"Coach Kelly, before I hired you, I called every head coach and administrator you'd worked for in the metroplex over the past 20 years. Each one said the same thing, you're confident, strong-willed, opinionated, assertive, and demanding of both staff and kids. But you're professional, have high expectations, and hold everyone accountable for progress. That's why I hired you. You'll be missed."

I thanked him for the compliment and told him I would miss the job too. The point of this story is simple: it's okay to be yourself.

Imagine the Possibilities

This message is for educators who use their positive will and determination to drive student achievement. Without vision and a plan, success is far less likely. I've worked with great teachers and coaches who shared their vision and set clear expectations.

My entire career was about believing in what seemed impossible. I once took over as head football coach at a school that had only won two games in the previous ten years. The community had given up on the program. During spring offseason, we took team photos, printed calendars with the game schedule, and invited everyone to attend.

That weekend, we loaded the team onto two buses and visited all five communities in the school district. Coaches and players went door to door, introduced themselves, and left a calendar at each home, 1,500 in total.

That fall, about 1,500 fans showed up for the first home game. We finished the season 2-8, still building toward success. Three years later, we hosted the district championship game in front of 12,000 fans. It was standing-room only, with people five rows deep along the fences. We won in the fourth quarter, 27-21. When the final whistle blew, the place erupted. My knees buckled as Gatorade poured down my back.

In the beginning, no one imagined this outcome. But I believed in the possibility, and that belief made it real. It's a memory everyone who was there will carry for life.

I dwell in possibility.

-Emily Dickinson

The Values of Competition

For me, there's no substitute for competition. It teaches invaluable lessons through both victory and defeat.

Defeat reveals the importance of determination, learning from mistakes, sportsmanship, teamwork, inner strength, self-reflection, and accountability.

Victory fosters confidence, positive thinking, pride, humility, respect, and a deepened sense of unity.

One thing is certain: the true value of competition should never be underestimated.

Real courage is when you know you're licked before you begin, but you begin anyway and see it through no matter what.

Listen to Your Gut

I've often written about the inner voice and spiritual strength we all carry. We are born with an instinct to sense the positive or negative energy of others. Some choose to ignore it, but as an educational leader, I made my best decisions by staying attuned to it.

In roles that required me to hire, promote, or occasionally terminate staff, I relied heavily on my gut. Before making any major decision, I'd say a prayer, take a deep breath, weigh the pros and cons, and sometimes seek an outside opinion.

If my inner voice felt at peace, I moved forward. If not, I paused and reconsidered.

Walking Through the Fire

As many of you know, I've served diligently and purposefully as an educational leader for most of my life. I've experienced incredible highs and spiritually challenging lows, but through it all, I never doubted God's plan — Jeremiah 29:11.

I'm reminded of September 11, 2001. At the time, I was an administrator at a middle school with 1,600 students. The librarian radioed me urgently to come to the library. I brought the department heads with me.

When we arrived, she pointed us toward the big-screen TV. The first tower had just collapsed. Smoke and debris filled the screen. The second tower was in flames. For a few minutes, we stood in stunned silence.

My inner voice took over. I said a silent prayer for strength, took a deep breath, grabbed the radio, and called our emergency team to my office. It included administrators, our campus police officer, two counselors, the school nurse, head custodian, and secretaries.

I explained what we'd seen. Not knowing the full extent of the attacks, we decided to quietly lock down the school. Instead of declaring a Code Blue (our highest alert), we opted for Code Green. Teachers locked their doors, no passes were issued, bells were silenced, and classes continued without interruption. We moved the police cruiser to block the main entrance. Administrators cleared hallways, staff monitored exits, and within minutes, the school was secured.

I announced Code Green over the intercom and called the superintendent's office to inform them of our status. About 90 minutes later, reports of additional terrorist attempts began to surface. Our phone lines were flooded with calls from concerned parents.

After careful discussion, we decided to lift the lockdown and return to the adjusted class schedule. There would be critiques and questions about my actions that day, but my top priority was, and always will be, the safety of students and staff.

Looking back, some may say our response was excessive. But at that moment, we were walking through the fire with limited information. That day is etched in my memory forever.

Self-Discipline

As a professional educator, you are bound to face a variety of situations that challenge your mental and emotional strength. With practice and intentional effort, you can prepare yourself for these moments by relying on self-discipline, the ability to gather and control your thoughts in stressful or difficult situations. Start by taking a few deep breaths, saying a silent prayer for strength, clearing your mind of distractions, and putting on your empathetic and understanding hat. Try to remain objective when making decisions.

When I was an athletic director and head coach, I had a great right tackle whose grandfather was not only the president of our athletic booster club but also the community fire chief, and a close personal friend. One Friday afternoon, just after lunch, he stopped by my office to check in and make sure everyone was ready for the game. We greeted each other with a hug, shared some small talk, and he said he was heading home to spend time with his wife before kickoff.

A few minutes later, as I returned to my office to finalize game preparations, my phone rang. It was our transportation director, urgently asking me to come to the front of the school. He informed me there had been a major accident involving the fire chief.

I grabbed my keys, ran out the door, and drove straight to the scene. It turns out the Chief had tried to cross a major highway and was broadsided by a car going 60 mph. The life flight helicopter arrived around the same time I did. I walked over as they used the jaws of life to remove him from the vehicle. They placed him on a gurney, but he was already gone.

I stopped in my tracks, bowed my head, said a short prayer asking God to receive his soul, took a few deep breaths, and walked back to my truck. My inner voice reminded me of his grandson, my player. I headed back to the high school and went straight to the main office. I informed the principal and head counselor that the Chief had been life-flighted but was dead on arrival. I asked the principal to contact the boy's mother to inform her of the situation. I then asked the counselor to pull the student from class and bring him to my office, emphasizing that he shouldn't be told anything until his mother arrived.

Back in my office, I instructed my secretary to clear the surrounding area, hallways, offices, and classrooms. I didn't want anyone nearby when the young man received the news. Alone again, I prayed for strength and compassion for him and his family. It was one of those rare moments when tears streamed down my face. I wiped them away and composed myself emotionally.

A few minutes later, the boy's mother rushed into my office, tears in her eyes. She knew her father had been airlifted, but she didn't yet know the full extent. I sat her down and gently told her I had been at the scene when they pulled him from the wreck. She began to cry uncontrollably, and I put my arm around her. Through tears, she asked if I thought he would make it. It was then that I gently told her I believed he was already gone.

I won't describe the next few minutes, you can imagine them. Once she had gathered herself, she asked if her son knew. I explained that he was on his way to my office but likely didn't know yet. We agreed she should be the one to tell him, and she asked me to stay. Moments later, he arrived with the counselor, and his mother sat him down to break the news. It was not well received, and the rest is a blur.

I don't think anyone is ever truly prepared for something like that. But I credit my self-discipline, faith, and spiritual guidance for helping me stay grounded that day. I lost a close friend in a tragic accident and discovered that God had given me the strength to lead through it.

Self-discipline begins with the mastery of your thoughts. If you don't control what you think, you can't control what you do.

Have a Good Work/Life Balance

Mother Teresa had immense spiritual guidance and an unwavering commitment to healing human suffering. One of my favorite quotes from her is about the importance of family life.

As a lifelong educator, I know firsthand how difficult it can be to maintain a healthy work/life balance. I struggled with it for years, constantly being pulled between the needs of the students and staff I served and the needs of my own family. To be a dedicated teacher, coach, or administrator, you often have to commit long hours before school starts and well into the evening. I was usually the first one in and the last one out.

As a result, my family time often suffered. That's why I encourage young educators to approach this challenge with love and intentionality. I held my children as often as I could, showed them love at every opportunity, made it a point to attend all their important events, and listened to them when they needed me. They grew up knowing and accepting my commitment to guiding and supporting other people's children.

Being honest with them didn't solve everything, but it taught them about independence and self-reliance early in life. Now that I've retired, I long to spend more time with them and their families. But of course, they now have their own responsibilities and lives to manage, so yes, I guess you could say the roles have reversed!

If you want to change the world, go home and love your family.

-Mother Teresa

Be a Skilled Communicator and Manager

In all my years of experience, I viewed each new encounter as both interesting and challenging. As a leader, you must recognize that every person, whether a parent, student, or participant, matters. Some may annoy, disappoint, or challenge you, but many will also surprise, encourage, and support you. Success requires a variety of characters, knowledgeable supporters, and experienced communicators. I'm not suggesting you use people, but I am encouraging you to utilize the resources available to you. Be a skilled communicator and an effective manager. Stay open-minded about others' contributions to the cause, you never know, you might gain a few lifelong friends.

There is a purpose for everyone you meet. Some people come into your life to test you, some to teach you, some to use you, and some to bring out the very best in you.

Friendships Are Important

As a professional educator, you must choose your friends wisely. I've met thousands of good people along my journey. Many were more than acquaintances; some became true friends and colleagues. Several dozen I check on regularly. A few dozen share their families, goals, and accomplishments with me. And then, there's a handful of soulmates, friends who share inner thoughts and concerns about life. If you're reading this section, you likely know who you are. Some of you have been lifelong friends and confidants. I will forever be grateful that we've stood by one another through life's roller coaster ride.

A friend is one of the best things you can have, and one of the best things you can be.

-Winnie the Pooh

Learn to Understand, Don't Judge

As an experienced administrator, teacher, and coach, I learned early on that I wasn't well-equipped to make decisions that significantly impacted students' learning environments. I felt both inadequate and disappointed. So, I made my own education and development a priority. Three years later, I earned my Master's in Educational Administration and completed a thorough internship focused on problem-solving and priority assessment. A year after that, I got my first Athletic Director/Head Football Coach position.

It was then that I truly learned the difference between judgment and understanding. You must have compassion and a good listening ear to genuinely understand a situation. When you're in a role that requires policy enforcement, decisions are often already made, it becomes about compliance rather than insight. That's different from understanding. In the latter half of my career, I learned that my preference was to lead with understanding. As a leader, you are obligated to know the difference.

It's easy to judge.

It's more difficult to understand.

Understanding requires compassion, patience, and a willingness to believe that good hearts sometimes choose poor methods.

Through judging, we separate. Through understanding, we grow.

-Doe Zantamata

Steer Away from Political or Religious Beliefs

I'm a firm believer in facts and in keeping ideology and progressive sociology out of the classroom. We live in the greatest democratic republic in the world, with inalienable rights guaranteed by the Constitution and the Bill of Rights. However, it is *not* an educator's role to interpret these rights for students. Your personal beliefs don't belong in the classroom.

We are entrusted to shape students' minds with academic disciplines, not our own philosophies. It's the parents' role to guide their children's values and beliefs. As educators, we often serve many roles, sometimes even stepping in as a parental figure, but we must remain mindful of the boundaries. Always stay on your side of the line in the sand.

Make Your Opinion Count

I taught Government and Economics during the final years of my career. My classes were full of group discussions, diverse opinions, and cultural perspectives. I made it a priority to create a neutral, unbiased environment where students could explore political and economic topics from multiple angles.

My main emphasis was this: *Make your voice heard.* Participate in the democratic process. Go vote. Have an opinion. Stand by your convictions. Make your vote count for who you are and what you believe in. Every vote matters equally, including yours.

The best teachers are those who show you where to look, but don't tell you what to see.

Alexandra K. Trenfor

Perform with an Attitude

This lesson always makes me smile! And if you know me well, you're probably laughing too. I've always believed that you can't help others build confidence without injecting a little attitude. And yes, you can show good sportsmanship while having a competitive edge.

I'm not talking about trash-talking, finger-pointing, or stare-downs. I'm talking about walking onto the field with confidence, warming up with energy, firing up your teammates before play, and saying a prayer of gratitude before the game. I believe in looking your opponent in the eye and offering a respectful smile and nod. The message is clear: *I'm ready, and I respect the moment.* That's the attitude, *be all you can be.*

"Come On, You Chilidog"

There are countless young men and women I had the honor of teaching, coaching, or influencing, many of whom faced serious obstacles. Their adversity built their strength, will, and determination. Among the thousands, you won't find one who can say they ever saw me give up.

If you give up when you're discouraged, you miss the opportunity to build character and improve your craft. My favorite phrase when confronting a poor effort was: *"Come on, you Chilidog!"* It wasn't an insult, it was a firm, spirited reminder to give more, to dig deeper. Over the years, it became a rallying cry among my players, one rooted in respect and effort. A lack of effort signals giving up, and that's just not in my DNA.

Wait, what? I have an attitude?
No really? Who knew

Create Memories

If you coach or teach kids, you're in the business of creating memories. We never truly know which moments will stay with the ones we influence. I have so many memories of the coaches, teachers, parents, and students I've worked with.

I once coached a 5'7" Indonesian student whose father had fled to America during a time of political upheaval in his home country. Tragically, six months after arriving, his father died of a sudden heart attack. A year later, the boy moved to our community with his mother and three sisters.

On his first day at school, he found me in the hallway and introduced himself as a thrower, shot put and discus. He asked when we could start practicing since I was the throwing coach. I chuckled, introduced myself officially, and explained that I was currently coaching football, and in Texas, sports are seasonal. Track wouldn't start until January. He simply nodded and walked off. He was a true freshman.

When spring arrived and track season began, he showed up with videos of Olympic and international throwers. I watched them with him, and he told me he'd already been training on his own since our first meeting. He started the season throwing 41 feet in the shot and 110 feet in the discus. He worked harder than any athlete I've ever coached. By the end of the season, he won district in both events, throwing 51 feet in the shot and 140 in the discus.

By senior year, he qualified for the state meet in both events. He set school records: 61'3" in the shot and 185'6" in the discus. At the regional meet that year, he was champion in both. I took a photo of him on the awards stand at North Texas State University. He stood at 5'7" on the tallest podium step. The athlete on his left, in third place, was 6'8", and the one on his right, in second, was 6'7". Even standing a foot higher, they still looked down on him. It was a real David vs. Goliath moment.

He went on to college on a full-ride scholarship to throw. I'll always cherish that moment and never forget the experience.

A memory is a photograph taken by the heart to make a special moment last forever.

Follow Your Passion, Make a Difference

As a professional educator, my career took me to many places, and I can honestly say I enjoyed every moment. At 20, I was coaching part-time while attending school full-time to earn my degree.

One day, I met with an education professor, Dr. J.H. Law, to discuss my degree plan. We talked about my future. I admitted I wasn't sure about coaching, even though I was good at it. When he asked why, I told him I didn't think I could make enough money to support a family.

He laughed gently, then looked me in the eyes and said:

"Son, have faith. Our Heavenly Father will always provide for you and your family. You'll be surprised at the rewards He gives you when you serve His purpose. Just listen to your inner voice and follow His lead."

He invited me to pray with him. I bowed my head, and he offered a beautiful prayer for guidance and acceptance. As I left his office, I thanked him, and from that day forward, I dedicated myself to becoming the best teacher and coach I could be.

I finished my degree and followed his advice. To this day, I still find it hard to believe I got paid to work with other people's children. I loved the job so much, I might've done it for free.

First Impressions Can Be Deceptive

Never judge a book by its cover. This phrase is often used for a reason, first impressions can be misleading. While trusting your instincts have value, it's important not to rush to judgment.

As a leader, you must keep an open mind when assessing talent, skill, intellect, and those intangible qualities that can't be seen at a glance. You certainly can't measure someone's heart just by looking at them.

Rely on your experience, observation, and intuition to evaluate how someone fits into your program. Many people will surprise you with their heart, determination, and dedication.

Love what you wake up for every day. Do what you love, be where you want to be, and create beautiful memories for life. This journey is splendid; travel well.

Be Reassuring and Understanding

As an educational leader, you'll need the skill of reassurance in countless situations: death, serious illness, abuse, divorce, separation, failure, social anxiety, fear, anger, the list goes on. Sadly, these challenges affect not just students, but also staff, parents, and colleagues.

One moment stands out vividly. I was the athletic director and head football coach in a small rural district. We had recently hired a new high school principal, an experienced and highly professional woman. We quickly developed a strong working relationship based on mutual respect.

In the second semester, one of our school board members lost her husband suddenly. I had a good relationship with her and her daughter, who was our head cheerleader. I visited with both of them, shared my condolences, and assured them I'd attend the funeral.

The next day, during a meeting with the principal, she mentioned she wanted to come with me to pay her respects. I agreed but warned her it would be a "different" kind of funeral, very country.

When I arrived to pick her up, I had to do a double take. She looked stunning in a formal three-piece suit. I complimented her, and we drove to a small country church. As we stepped out, she laughed and admitted she might be overdressed. I smiled and nodded.

We took a seat in the sixth pew. When the casket was brought in, the principal leaned over, wide-eyed, and asked what kind of funeral this was. Behind the casket were 50–60 trophies with roosters mounted on top: no flowers, just trophies. The pallbearers were dressed in overalls, white T-shirts, straw hats, and cowboy boots.

I whispered that I'd explain on the way home.

After the service and a visit with the family, we got back in the car. I explained that the man made his living through cockfighting. He was known throughout five southern states and parts of Mexico as one of the best. Yes it was, and still is, illegal.

The principal was shocked but grateful we went. She was glad we showed support and empathy during a difficult time.

Soulmate

Do you believe in soulmates? Have you ever met someone who truly understood you? I believe we have the opportunity to meet a few soulmates throughout our lifetime. If you're in tune with your spiritual inner voice, you'll recognize one instantly. If not, you might miss the chance to connect with them.

Over my 65 years of life, I've had the privilege of recognizing a few kindred souls, one of whom is my current wife, the mother of my children.

The first was a man I met on a pavilion bench at Dollywood. He appeared out of nowhere and sat next to me. He immediately struck up a conversation about my depression and the physical pain I was experiencing from a recent open-heart surgery. He knew far more about what I was going through than anyone else. He saw my pain, and we prayed together for understanding and relief. Before I even raised my bowed head, he was already walking away. I never saw him again, but I still recognize him as a major factor in my recovery and spiritual recommitment.

The next soulmate was someone I met while attending graduate school. I was part of a professional crew who had gone back to school while working full-time. Our group, our little grad school posse, rolled into that first spring class with confidence and flair. Lol! As we walked through the door, I felt this inner voice speaking directly to my soul: "Y'all need to sit down and calm down." I recognized the message immediately and looked around the room to see where it was coming from. A few seconds later, I locked eyes with her. She gave me a subtle nod, and of course, I nodded back and sat down.

After class, I went over to introduce myself. She said my reputation had preceded me and then introduced herself. We took classes together for over two years. Our relationship was purely platonic, but the friendship we formed was lifelong. Over the years, we could communicate without technology, just a knowing understanding between two connected souls.

The third soulmate was a coach and friend who saw potential in me, not just as an athlete but as a person. I was a 14-year-old country boy with no direction at the time. He taught me to be determined, diligent, and self-disciplined. He was the first to show me how to recognize my inner voice and truly listen to it.

If you've read this far, let me leave you with something positive: Don't ignore the inner voice of connection. God sends soulmates to guide and encourage us through life's obstacles.

Your Perception Skills Matter

As an administrator, coach, and teacher, I had the opportunity to work with staff, parents, and kids. If you've been following my journey, you know I share my experiences to pass them along to the next generation of educators. My stories are meant to encourage the development of your ability to read others through body language, tone of voice, and facial expressions.

Once you get good at it, words become almost unnecessary. You can sense what someone is thinking or feeling just by observing. This skill gives you power, the power to understand and solve problems. It helps maintain relationships because you're not just hearing people, you're truly listening.

Perspective and Attitude

Most of life comes down to perspective and attitude. With time comes an undeniable opportunity for growth and change. When working with other people's children, you have choices. You can teach them about their potential and open doors for their future.

If people stopped looking for things that offended them and started looking for things that inspired them,
I'm sure we would have a better country.

Encourage Their Dreams: Be an inspiration.

Too many educators today focus on political ideologies and so-called "woke" introspection. This approach is creating a generation of defensive and confrontational young adults.

I believe an educator's role is to be objective, supportive, and uplifting. Be all that you can be and teach your students to do the same.

Passion Pays Off

Wow! I finally found an illustration that perfectly captures my thoughts on teaching and coaching! Aside from my children and grandchildren, some of my greatest accomplishments have come through influencing generations of young people.

I've said this before: I would've done it for free. But I was blessed and fortunate to help many students achieve personal and athletic success.

To all you young educators out there who share this passion: know that your efforts will be rewarded many times over. Your impact won't go unnoticed. Many of your students will follow you into fields of service, and their admiration will last a lifetime.

Love what you do. Do what you love.

The Volume of Your Voice

I have to laugh at this one! My wife and family remind me all the time about the volume of my voice.

After four decades of administration, teaching, and coaching, I developed different "octaves" of communication. If you're a young educator, prepare yourself, this is coming.

In an auditorium, on a field, or in a classroom, volume and clarity are your friends. A commanding voice helps you hold attention. For some reason, many kids have a hard time respecting a softer, meeker tone. But an authoritative, direct, and booming voice usually does the trick.

Over time, I developed three main octaves:

1. **Conversational**: soft, for one-on-one or casual settings.

2. **Direct/Instructive**: clear and firm, perfect for the classroom.

3. **Boisterous/Commanding**: loud and precise, for the field or gym.

Here's the challenge: sometimes your brain forgets to switch back to the quieter tone in calmer settings. So my advice? Be mindful of your environment, and adjust your voice accordingly!

Travel the Road of Your Passion

I believe the road to success varies across schools and districts. Some leaders prefer direction over diversity. Some believe in culling talent, while others believe in cultivating it. Some encourage paying for tutors and clubs, while others invest time in teaching leadership and skills during the off-season. These are distinct paths to career success.

I chose a road that was neither privileged nor predetermined, a road that encouraged building relationships alongside skill development. Talent is important, but it isn't exclusive to the financially well-off. Many economically disadvantaged kids have incredible talent. They just need a caring, devoted professional to believe in them. That's the path I chose for my career, and it has been a great ride!

Personal Health

Those who know me can attest that I've faced many physical and emotional challenges in adulthood. My journey has been enlightening, exciting, and at times, exhausting. I must admit, though, it has taken a toll on my health. Retirement has only delayed the progression of some conditions.

This lesson isn't about my health, it's about paying attention to yours. I truly believe you can be a passionate, dedicated educational leader while also being mindful of your own well-being. It takes intention and an attitude of self-care. Many of you know my story and my commitment. Let it serve as a reminder: take care of yourself, too.

I kept going because I didn't have any
other choice- it was either fail or fly.
So when you ask me how I learned to fly,
 I'll tell you the story of how I found my wings.
Maybe it's not a story of beauty and victory,
but it's one that's all me and very real.

Know Your Purpose, Be Thankful

Early in my career as an Athletic Director and Head Football Coach, I had a life-altering experience during a varsity game. That experience led to a lifesaving open-heart surgery.

While awaiting the procedure, I had an adverse reaction to a Nitro IV drip and slipped into a coma for several hours. During that time, I had a vivid experience: I saw a bright light and heard a voice say, "You must go back. There are many things left for you to do. It's not your time." I instantly woke up. That moment stayed with me, even as I questioned its reality in the months that followed.

That was 30 years ago. Today, I know with certainty that the Lord spoke to me that day. Seven weeks after surgery, I returned to work: renewed, dedicated, and committed to making a difference. I've since had thousands of opportunities to impact the lives of students and young educators.

This past year, we were blessed with our grandson Wyatt. He's stolen my rebuilt heart, and I believe he is part of the reason I was called back to life. I thank God for him, and for all of life's blessings, in my daily prayers. I believe in Jesus and His forgiveness, and I know it's part of His plan for me. If you believe the same, I'm glad. If not, know that you're in my prayers.

Let Your Word Be Your Bond

If you've followed me, you know I'm a firm believer that your word is your bond. When I give you my word, it's a solemn promise, one that puts my credibility and reputation on the line.

As an agent of cultural change, there were many times early on when all I had to offer was my word. To young teachers and coaches: your word matters. Students are watching and listening. Don't underestimate the power of keeping your word, it's the foundation of strong, lasting relationships.

Managing Your Stress

As a professional educator, I must acknowledge the serious impact stress has on long-term health. As a young administrator, teacher, and coach, I used to think stress was just a sign of weakness. I ignored the toll that long hours, intense pressure, and constant demands were taking on me.

After 15 years, my health declined, and I was diagnosed with cardiovascular disease. I had open-heart surgery and wrestled with how this could happen so young. Doctors explained that part of it was genetic, but not all. Through recovery and support, I came to understand that part of the issue was me.

That's when I realized job stress, defined as the emotional or mental strain caused by adverse or demanding circumstances, is real. It's not a myth. It's something that needs to be acknowledged and addressed.

I'll never forget a coaching friend who once showed up at my house, unannounced, just to tell me I should quit and do something else. He meant well, and we're still close today. But I chose to continue, wiser, but still direct and honest.

I had to learn to let go of things. To say what needed to be said and then move on. Easier said than done, but with support and effort, I made the change. I was able to serve for another 25 years with only minor health issues.

If you're a young educational leader, pace yourself. Find a way to release stress, whether it's through prayer, hobbies, exercise, or time with loved ones. Your longevity depends on it.

You can't win.

They tell you to speak how you feel, then tell you that you're too much.

Then when you finally break, they ask why you bottled it up.

Be an Influencer

If you follow my insights regularly, you know how much I value my influence on those I teach, coach, or supervise. Influence is the capacity to affect the character, development, or behavior of someone or something. My daily approach reflects these values. If you are a young teacher or coach, **never** underestimate your ability to influence your participants. You play a vital role in shaping their development and expectations.

Hard Work, Determination, and Preparation

Some people let life happen to them; others make life happen for them. As a professional educator, I chose to demonstrate that life is what you make of it. Yes, there will be obstacles and bumps along the way. But I taught that hard work, determination, and preparation provide the tools to navigate those challenges. Stay positive and creative when facing adversity. View these moments as opportunities to learn and grow. Each is a chance to strengthen your character.

Life doesn't give free lessons to anyone. So, when I say life taught me, rest assured that I PAID THE PRICE.

Educational Options for All

I believe all kids can learn. Education is a powerful tool for progress. But not every student needs, or wants, to attend college. Unfortunately, decades ago, America largely phased out vocational and technical training in public schools. Now, many young people must pay for this education after high school. Yet careers in plumbing, mechanics, nursing, welding, drafting, carpentry, and similar trades offer excellent pay and long-term success. We must fully restore these paths in our public education system.

Persistent Mastermind

This next thought rings true more often than not: people often have perceptions about what I bring to the table in creating success. But when they begin to see what it really takes, many raise their eyebrows in surprise. And when those goals are finally reached, they often just shrug and smile, now understanding the effort behind the results.

Professional Responsibility

Wow! Nearly every supervisor I've worked under, superintendents, principals, athletic directors, head coaches, trainers, told me I expected too much from students and colleagues. But when success followed, they stood proudly beside me. I've had many successes, and I didn't measure them in wins alone. Success comes in many forms.

There will be people who love the idea of you, but lack the maturity to handle the reality of you.

There Is a Purpose for Your Life

After several near-death experiences over the past two decades, I know God was not ready for me yet. He still had a purpose for me and a plan for my influence. Every night, I thank Him for the day and promise to live the next with purpose. I urge you to let God use you to positively impact the lives of others.

Somebody didn't wake up today, but you did. That's enough reason to stop complaining, and that's enough to be thankful for. Never let your troubles blind you to your daily blessings.

Never Look Back in Envy, Look Forward to Possibility

If I could have taught this lesson to my younger self, I would have found more peace much earlier. For various reasons, my career was often in transition, from one team, school, or job to another. Still, I built many meaningful relationships and memories. A close friend once told me: *"Never look back in envy. Look forward to endless possibilities."* That was wise advice, and I've taken it to heart.

To be happy, you must: Let go of what's gone. Be grateful for what remains. Look forward to what is coming next.

Look Forward to New Experiences

Wow! This phrase captures exactly how I felt every time I stepped into a new job; there were many. Patience was a skill I had to work hard to develop. Maturity came over time. I hope your lessons in patience are gentler than mine have been.

The new is already here. The old is just making a lot of noise, dying.

Caring and Sharing

For over 40 years, as an educator and coach, I've focused on helping students and athletes discover their purpose in life. I encouraged them to explore their passions, goals, and personal values. Back then, I'm not sure they always understood the purpose behind it. But now, many have grown with their own families, and some have reached out to say *thank you*. They get it now.

We are all here for some special reason. Stop being a prisoner of your past. Become the architect of your future.

-Robin S. Sharma

Forgiveness Is Imperative

Life is too short to hold grudges. I believe deeply in forgiveness, though not necessarily in forgetting. Our failures and hardships often teach us our greatest lessons. In life, you can usually count on one hand the number of true, lifelong friendships. Treasure those.

Tupac once said...

"Just because you lost me as a friend doesn't mean you gained me as an enemy. I'm bigger than that. I still wanna see you eat, just not at my table."

I Believe in Possibilities

As a teacher and coach, the following poem expresses what I believe about possibilities. I've shared this concept with thousands of young people. America is a land of opportunity, you can be anything you set your heart on. With hard work, a positive attitude, and persistence, you can achieve your dreams.

Determined Pathway

I learned this lesson as a teenager trying to find my way. I was the best football player in the county, a strong student, a youth leader at church, and had a personal relationship with Jesus. There were conflicts, bad influences, and people who didn't believe in me. But I realized early on that my success couldn't depend on popularity or others' opinions. That determination has stayed with me throughout life, and I've tried to pass it on.

Either people like you, or they don't. Never try to convince someone of your worth. If they can't appreciate you, they don't deserve you. Respect yourself and surround yourself with people who value you.

Focus on the Light at the End of the Tunnel

Adversity and hardship are part of life and competition. When building programs and fostering teamwork, it's essential to teach the value of hard work, determination, and spiritual strength. These qualities help us endure the dark times and keep our eyes on the light ahead. The struggle is real, but so is the reward. As the light grows closer and brighter, our confidence and sense of achievement grow with it.

The light at the end of the tunnel may be an oncoming train.

Climbing Out of a Culture

Growing up as a country boy, I never had the luxury of thinking I was better than anyone else. My family was rich in love and respect but financially struggling. By the age of 11, I was already working. I took jobs on farms, ranches, and in agriculture all the way through my senior year of high school. Academics and football gave me the opportunity to play college ball and earn a degree. I didn't have the time to "sway and play" like many of my college buddies. I understood the value of education and the sacrifices required to achieve both personal and professional goals. Even then, I knew I was different from most others my age.

Be the Artist, Mold the Clay

This, I believe with all my heart, the young people we teach, coach, and mentor are like unshaped clay. They rely on us to help instill proper values, behaviors, and high expectations. They come from a variety of economic and social backgrounds, but we must look past these differences to ensure that each child has an equal opportunity to grow. That makes us, as educators, agents of change and hope. I truly believe that all kids can learn and thrive under the right guidance.

Never judge the future of a person based on their present situation because time has the power to change any black coal into a shiny diamond.

Chasing the Dream

I'll admit it, I'm guilty of chasing dreams. I never concerned myself with other people's perceptions, nor did I go out of my way to please them. Growing up poor in the national forest, I was determined to rise above my circumstances. With good grades and the support of teachers and coaches, I excelled. When the chance came to play college football and earn my degree, I stepped forward and never looked back. I pursued my dreams relentlessly. The road wasn't always smooth, but I've enjoyed 40 incredible years doing what I love. Honestly, I still can't believe people paid me to do something I might have done for free.

Live life like someone left the gate open.

Memories – A Window to the Soul

We rarely pause to appreciate the many extraordinary moments that come with working with other people's children. Yet we often remember the tough times more vividly. I can still recall my one and only 0–10 season, but the first championship team I coached has faded in memory. Still, those memories are priceless. Last year, we had a 30-year reunion of that championship team, with most of the players, their wives, some parents, and all the coaches. As the head coach, I felt truly honored. I was overwhelmed by emotion, but grateful for the chance to reconnect. Take the time to slow down and savor these moments, memories truly are windows to the soul.

Different from All the Rest

I knew from a young age that God had a purpose for my life. My teenage years were filled with questions and searching, but I followed the lead of His Spirit to places I never imagined. I left the small-town life that defined my family at 18 and worked hard labor jobs to pay for college, never once taking out a student loan. I kept my faith and trusted God's plan. With hard work, determination, and passion, I pursued my craft, teaching and coaching, and became an athletic director and head football coach at 26. At that time, I was the youngest person in the state to hold that position. I knew then, as I know now, that I was different.

Humble to know
I'm not better than anybody,
butwise enough to know
I'm different from the rest.

Carry Your Own Sword

You can always be caring, concerned, and devoted to those you serve. I was committed and supportive as an educator, but I learned to remain cautious. When working with the public, remember that most people are ultimately looking out for themselves and their families, as they should. But serving without considering your own needs and health will only lead to burnout and disappointment. You carry your own sword, so never lose sight of your own well-being. Sometimes, you'll be the only one standing up for what's right.

Love everybody.

But never sell your sword.

-Paulo Coelho

Accept the End, Welcome the Next Challenge

If you haven't yet reached the end of a job, you eventually will. I had to learn that the hard way. When your work is your passion, it becomes part of your spirit, and it's hard to accept that your intent or passion is misunderstood, or no longer wanted. The first time that happens, it dims your inner light. But don't dwell on the loss. Rely on your faith and inner strength to move forward. There will be another opportunity, God promises in 2 Corinthians 4:16–18 to renew our spirits. In my 35-year career across 10 schools, I left most positions by choice, though in a few cases, leadership moved on without me. Either way, I went on to succeed at the next stop. Just be faithful and obedient.

Learn to be done. Not mad, not bothered, just done. Protect your peace at all cost.

Hold On to Your Truth

I don't impose my views, nor do I twist facts to suit a narrative. Most people don't think like I do; I tend to see things as they really are. Yes, I believe in hope and divine intervention. But truth is truth, and facing reality is the only way to bring about real change. I won't share my truth unless you ask for it. But when you do, be ready. I won't sugarcoat it, and anyone who knows me well can vouch for that.

If you don't want the truth, don't ask me.

If you want something sugar-coated, go eat a donut.

Age Gracefully

There comes a time in everyone's career when they reach a crossroads. You know the one, your mind says you've done it a million times, but your body warns there will be consequences if you try it again. The message is unwelcome, so you push through it to complete the task. Then you spend the next two weeks recovering.

At my age, that's what finally pushed me into retirement. I don't miss the long hours or the pain, but I do miss the relationships I built and the time spent helping kids grow. Many still keep in touch, some now teachers and coaches themselves. They call during their seasons, seeking advice on strategy on personnel.

My wife says I should start a consulting business, but I could never charge anyone for knowledge that others freely passed on to me. I'm just trying to age gracefully, giving back as I grow older.

I have reached an age where my mind says. "I can do that," my body says, "try it and you'll be sorry."

Validation – A Byproduct of Your Efforts

As professional educators, our goal is to help kids learn, grow, and mature in preparation for life's challenges. It's more than reading, writing, and arithmetic. It's more than X's and O's, hard work, and winning.

It's about caring, listening, guiding, and setting expectations. When you build strong relationships and help students define their life goals, you don't need external validation. The validation comes naturally, through karma, through impact, through the quiet reward of knowing you followed your inner voice. That alone is enough.

Plan for the Ineffable Experience

Have you ever had an ineffable experience in your career? They're rare, and often come after beating long odds. I've had a few.

Like winning a district championship at a school that hadn't had a winning season in over a century. Or winning in track at a school that didn't even have a track. Or turning a discipline plan around, from 97 fights in one semester to just one the next year.

Helping 28 students, all of whom had failed the TAKS test twice, pass and graduate. These moments lit up my soul.

Of course, I've faced adversity too. But I lean on those amazing student successes. They remind me why I did this work.

ineffable

(adj) too great to be expressed in words

Daily Positive Attitude

If I could give my younger self one piece of advice, it would be this: protect your peace.

If you're from a younger generation, take this to heart, happiness may be fleeting at times, but a daily positive attitude creates more joyful moments in the long run. Try to enjoy the journey and the experiences life offers.

Help Them Grow Their Wings

As a leader, I've learned that staff, teachers, students, and athletes sometimes need space to grow. Over the years, I've watched many spread their wings and fly on their own.

A good leader anticipates this and supports it. Though it's hard to let go of those who have become vital to the team, it's necessary to encourage their growth. No replacement will fill their shoes exactly, but life moves on, and so must we.

No one is irreplaceable. Not even you.

NEVER Let Them See You Sweat

When faced with controversy or adversity, don't hang your head in doubt or frustration.

Take a deep breath, lift your head high, and say a quiet prayer for strength and wisdom. Then act with purpose and confidence.

NEVER let your adversaries see you sweat. God is always with you — **Philippians 4:13**.

If your path demands you walk through Hell, walk like you own the place.

BUILDING FOR SUCCESS

Impose a Spirit of Determination

Let's talk a little about determination as a factor in success. Mental preparation and a positive attitude are essential components. Some people are naturally inclined to have these qualities, but not many are. As a leader, you must set the example. I like to call it my *will* or *desire*; it burns within me constantly. You should know that you can, and should, influence your participants to develop this spirit as well. When these qualities are combined with hard work, real progress toward goals is inevitable.

Those who impose their will and refuse to accept the challenges the mountain poses will eventually conquer it...keep winning!

\- *Coach Corey*

Progress and Patience

Instant gratification is a myth, most of the time. When building a program, the leader must understand that progress comes from consistent hard work, extraordinary effort, and daily determination. Achievements occur in small increments, slow and steady. For a leader, quitting is not an option. I find it hard to respect someone who isn't willing to finish what they've started. Strength and confidence are built by pushing through difficult times.

It won't happen overnight
But if you quit.
It won't happen at all

Stick With the Plan

As an agent of change, the leader must move with both focus and urgency, while recognizing that the process takes time. Rome wasn't built in a day. Even with a great attitude, positive reinforcement, and clear direction, patience and pacing is essential. A leader must have a plan and cultivate a circle of influence. Most importantly, they must build trust-based relationships with both parents and participants. These relationships will be critical as the leader moves forward. There is much work to do in a limited time, so pace yourself and stick to the plan.

The man who moves a mountain begins by carrying away small stones.

- *Confucius*

Persistence Leads to Quiet Successes

I've always taught my athletes that talk is cheap, but hard work and persistence lead to quiet, meaningful successes. Let your performance speak on the field, court, diamond, or track. As a coach, I had no patience for showboating. My players and coaching staff understood there was a standard of conduct, one that required humility and respect for opponents. Respect is earned, and disrespect only takes us backward.

When people laugh at you, don't react, don't feel down. Wake up the lion inside you. Work hard in silence.
Let your success make the noise.

Credibility: Pulling the Wagon

Early in my career, I learned that to be a true leader, you must be willing to take the lead and set the example. Many within your circle of influence may doubt your expectations or resist your influence. Some may even work against you out of jealousy or insecurity. Don't be naïve, identify them clearly. Make an honest effort to bring them on board, but don't get distracted by their negativity. Always remember, staff, colleagues, parents, and athletes are watching. Your credibility is constantly on the line. No one will follow you if you don't say what you mean and mean what you say. Don't be a hypocrite.

Hypocrites are those who apply to others the standards that they refuse to accept for themselves.

- *Noam Chomsky*

Your Word Is Your Bond

As a professional educator for nearly 40 years, I learned early on not to make promises to kids lightly. My word was my bond. If you're a young teacher or coach, understand that your credibility is on the line every time you give your word. Say what you mean, and mean what you say. Avoid making promises you may not be able to keep. Instead, instill expectations and a strong work ethic, those will lead to real achievements. Be a good listener. Offer options and possible solutions. Show genuine concern and emotion. But remember: if you do make a promise, follow through. I've made my share over the years. Most worked out, but some required real effort and accountability. Be careful and weigh the risks.

Don't take it so seriously
that you forget to have fun.

Yes, you can have balance and joy

Cultivate a Climate of Loyalty

Loyalty is essential to building a strong team, especially among staff and parents within your inner circle. Those who know me well recognize that I'm a straight shooter. They also know I'm human, and I've made my share of mistakes. As a leader, your inner circle must be bonded by loyalty. But loyalty does not mean blind obedience. True respect allows for concern and constructive disagreement. Loyalty means standing together, even when asking tough questions. As a leader, you must be open to those conversations.

Loyalty means I am down with you whether you are wrong or right. But I will tell you when you are wrong and help you get it right.

Exemplify and Demand Humility

There's something powerful about humility. As an athletic director, head coach, and teacher, I encouraged those under my guidance to be confident and committed to success. It's a core pillar of any strong program. But I drew the line at showboating, trash talk, negative gestures, or intimidation. Act like you've been there before, and celebrate with your teammates, not at someone else's expense. It's frustrating to watch acts of arrogance on television during games. So many intelligent, educated individuals display arrogance without thought. What happened to valuing hard work and humility?

I hate when people confuse education with having a bachelor's degree and still be an idiot.

Be a Positive Role Model

If you're a young teacher or coach, never underestimate the impact you have on the young men you serve. Like it or not, we are often parent figures to them. That's why it's so important to model and teach confidence, character, commitment, and compassion. Emphasize the value of respect, while also reinforcing the importance of discipline. These young people need to know how much you care, and believe that you truly want the best for them.

I had father figures. I had an older brother. I had coaches. I had teachers. I had community fathers. I want to become that person that was doing those things for me.

Model Appropriate Behavior

If you know me at all, then you know I strive to be a peacemaker. Of course, my name, Michael Patrick Kelly, reflects the legacy of two patron saints (Saint Michael and Saint Patrick). And with the last name Kelly, my Irish heritage suggests a short temper, a stubborn streak, and a certain bullheadedness! That combination can be a challenge. I try to avoid conflict, but if pushed, I'll roll up my sleeves and engage. Life hasn't always been easy because of these traits, but I've learned to temper them over time. As an educational leader, I came to understand that modeling appropriate behavior is essential. When everyone is watching your every move, you must carefully adjust your responses in critical situations. Stop, take a deep breath, assess the situation, and stay calm. Learning to do this can help you avoid complications down the road.

Walk a mile to avoid a fight, but when one starts, don't back down an inch.

Planning and Preparation Are Essential

This is a crucial lesson for new administrators, teachers, and coaches. You may have many great ideas about what you want to accomplish, but good intentions are no substitute for solid preparation and organization. From the first day of in-service to the winter break, time will move at breakneck speed. Plan ahead. Stay at least a week in front of the rush. Ask questions, and find a reliable mentor to guide you. Be early to every meeting, never late. Take notes, and no matter how exhausted you are, stay alert. The first year in a new role can be overwhelming as you get your footing. Remember, you're not alone, many others on staff are going through the same thing. Take it one day at a time and stay positive. Kids can easily pick up on your insecurity.

When you are overwhelmed, remember: a little at a time is how you it gets done. One thing. One task. One moment at a time.

Conquering Anxiety

Years ago, Stephen Curry was an afterthought in the NBA draft. But through relentless hard work, he became the leader of a championship team and one of the most recognizable players in the league. In a statement he once made, he acknowledged struggling with pregame anxiety, something many athletes, test-takers, actors, and educators experience. Curry credits his preparation: hours spent lifting weights, running the court, and shooting thousands of baskets in solitude. That practice helped him overcome anxiety and perform with confidence. If you're a young administrator, teacher, or coach, a big part of your role is to help others prepare for and manage their anxieties. Practice may not make perfect, but it does make performance possible, and often exceptional.

I've never been afraid of big moments. I get butterflies. I get nervous and anxious, but I think those are all good signs that I'm ready for the moment.

-   Stephen Curry

Overcoming Your Fear

Fear is something we all face, even from an early age. It's a powerful force that can affect performance, both in the classroom and on the field. It can grip your heart and cloud your perception. One way to overcome fear is through preparation, hard work, and building confidence. The stronger you become, mentally and physically, the more consistent and resilient your performance will be. The second way is through faith. As **2 Timothy 1:7** reminds us, "God has not given us a spirit of fear, but of power, love, and a sound mind." As a leader, you must set the example, help your participants face fear and rise above it.

Everything you have ever wanted is on the other side of fear.

- George Adair

The Power of Visualization

Visualization is a powerful mental tool. As a teacher and coach, I regularly used it as a strategy, training students to mentally rehearse success from start to finish. Visualization helps calm nerves and build confidence. I once taught a class of 28 students who had previously failed the state-required TAKS test in World History. I had them for just three months before their final retake. When another professional administered the test, 27 passed, 16 with commended scores (missing no more than three of the 49 questions). The only student who failed had rarely attended class. Visualization was one of the key techniques I used, and it worked. The power of the mind should never be underestimated.

Make your vision so clear that your fear becomes irrelevant.

Excellence for Life

If you're a young teacher or coach, understand that managing your classroom or arena is only the beginning. Preparation and organization lay the groundwork for order, but your ultimate goal should be to influence participants to develop confidence, character, compassion, and a commitment to excellence. Your leadership helps instill values that will guide them into adulthood. You have the power to make a lasting difference.

Management is focusing on getting someone to get a result. Leadership is producing a standard in someone that, when you're gone, they will live by to produce higher-level results consistently.

Good Players – Better Humans

I always emphasized to my players that football, like any sport, eventually ends for everyone. That's why my focus was on helping them grow into good teammates, sons, brothers, and citizens. I wanted them to understand that what they take away from the game should serve them far beyond it.

You can win, win, win, but if you're not equipping young men to be great husbands and fathers, you lose.

- *Dabo Swinney*

Nurture Their Talents and Genius

If this isn't your ultimate goal as an educator, then you may be in the wrong profession. You should have a genuine interest in every student or athlete you influence. Discover their passions. Identify their strengths. Encourage their efforts and support their dreams. Highlight their potential. Children need affirmation, support, and belief. You must want to help them become difference-makers.

Awaken what's already within

If each person has natural gifts and innate talents, then the true nature of education must involve the awakening, inviting, and blessing of the inner genius and unique life spirit of each young person.

Plant Your Feet Firmly on the Ground

This lesson is often best learned the hard way. When you're a successful player or coach, it's difficult to ignore all the compliments and constant praise. As success becomes more frequent, it's crucial to shift your focus to the concept of "we." Remember how you got there, success is rarely a solo achievement. Believe in yourself, but don't forget that you're one of many. To reach the top and stay there, a leader must keep the entire team motivated and committed to progress.

Humility is not low self-esteem. Humility is low self-preoccupation.

Make the Investment in Them

Good coaches never forget this truth: our players are people first. Always treat them with respect, dignity, and honor. They need to know that you care, and they will remember your care and integrity long after their playing days are over.

You don't win with Xs and Os. What you win with is people.

- *Joe Gibbs*

Execute the Plan

This is a critical lesson for young educators. Knowledge, preparation, and planning are essential to building a successful program. These foundational elements shape a positive outcome, but the most important part is execution. Your credibility depends on it. And it cannot be done alone. Execution must be a team effort, involving your staff and supportive community. When everyone works together, success is inevitable.

The magic is in the execution of the plan...not a magic plan.

Recognize and Develop the Talent

As a professional educator and coach, I realized early on that it was my responsibility to evaluate and assess the talent level of every participant. There are many ways to do this, and it takes time to collect all the necessary information. Once that process is complete, you can create a plan that fosters skill development and expands knowledge. You must believe, along with your staff, that each individual can grow, improve, and fulfill their potential.

Everyone is gifted, but some people never open their package. It is foolish to believe that you are insignificant. We are treasure chests with more jewels inside than we can imagine.

Don't Punch the Clock

As a professional educator, I felt a personal responsibility to show up early and bring a positive attitude every day. Staff and students, especially students, can sense insincerity and negativity from a mile away. I loved working with and helping them, which is why I was often the first to arrive and the last to leave. It wasn't about outworking anyone else; it was about being available when I was needed most. If you're more focused on the clock and what's for dinner than your calling, this may not be the right profession for you.

Your mind is like a garden. What grows there is up to you. You can grow flowers or you can grow weeds.
We all reap what we sow, so let's decide to sow what is good.

Teamwork Makes the Dream Work

As a building administrator, athletic director, and head coach, my greatest challenge was always getting everyone on the same page. I began by emphasizing teamwork. My goal was to downplay the "me" mentality and reinforce the power of "we." I focused on the strength of the group and the weakness of individualism. When things go wrong, everyone feels the impact. When things go right, success is shared. I made it a priority to design daily scenarios and activities to strengthen teamwork. As a leader, you must make time to intentionally build these skills.

Teamwork is the ability to work together toward a common vision. The ability to direct individual accomplishments toward organizational objectives. It is the fuel that allows common people to attain uncommon results.

Developing Team Skills

This lesson is for young teachers and coaches who aspire to have long, impactful careers. Relying solely on talented players to build a successful team is a mistake. A winning team requires your knowledge, determination, and leadership. None of us begin with all these qualities, we earn them through mentorship, educational clinics, and coaching camps. Ask questions. Build relationships. Join professional networks. Commit to learning the skills and strategies that will set you apart. Once you've done that, you'll be able to develop players at every level. Your goal should be to guide the most talented to greatness, push the good players to be even better, and help the average ones become solid contributors. When you reach this level of leadership, you'll be a respected and sought-after teacher and coach.

Any coach can recruit an athlete, but a real coach can develop one.

No Individual Is More Important Than the Team

I once had a junior running back who rushed for over 2,000 yards, but he became too full of himself. While we had high hopes for a strong season, his attitude became a problem. He skipped class, disrespected the team, and let his ego get in the way. After a home visit with his parents, we all agreed he would turn things around. But within a week, the principal called me into her office. The student had not upheld his end of the agreement, and she scheduled a meeting with all his teachers, his parents, and me. Each teacher voiced concerns, and I reiterated that my expectations were clear: our players are students first, athletes second.

The principal gave him an ultimatum: attend class on time and make an effort, or be removed from the team.

After the meeting, we joined the team at practice. The player took his place in the huddle, ran a basic play incorrectly, and when asked to repeat it, deliberately made the same mistake. When my assistant coach confronted him, the player lashed out, cursing and pointing fingers. That was the breaking point.

I blew the whistle and stopped the entire practice. I asked the athletic trainer to bring the equipment cart. The player removed his gear, down to his gym shorts and t-shirt, and placed it in the cart. I told him, in front of the entire team, that he was off the team. The trainer escorted him to the field house to collect his personal belongings. He was no longer welcome in our facility.

I then addressed the team. I made it clear that respect for the staff and each other was non-negotiable. No one player is more important than the team. That season, our team played with heart and unity. Without our "star" running back, they proved that winning comes from collective effort. He missed out on a great experience because he didn't respect the team, and the team rose to the occasion without him.

Sometimes you gotta put aside what you feel for them, and pay attention to what their action are saying they feel for you.

Bumps in the Road

Most leaders engage in extensive planning, preparation, and implementation before launching a new program. Being organized and well-prepared is always better. However, you must understand that unexpected bumps in the road are inevitable. These obstacles offer leaders valuable opportunities to learn and adjust. Don't get frustrated, use your intellect and determination to find solutions.

If everything was perfect, you would never learn and you would never learn and you would never grow.

Evaluation and Correction

As an administrator, teacher, and coach, I always emphasized the value of evaluation, performance review, and learning from mistakes. We often used video analysis, data, and statistics for this purpose. These tools played a crucial role in growth and improvement. Enhancing performance and building confidence are hallmarks of a skilled educator committed to advancing both the group and the individual.

What do you do with a mistake? Recognize it, admit it, learn from it, forget it.

-Dean Smith

Success Is a Product of Attitude

This is a life lesson I've passed on to my own children. It's also part of the armor I carry as a leader. When you're at the helm and implementing various aspects of your program, you will face roadblocks. These challenges test your inner strength and determination.

Since your staff, students, and athletes are watching, your responses must be measured, positive, and purposeful. As you overcome each obstacle, you demonstrate the power of perseverance. Success is never automatic, it is always the result of attitude and effort.

Fall down seven times, stand up eight.

Effort as a Barometer

I've mentioned effort as a key component in reaching goals, but it's also a powerful barometer for gauging a staff member's alignment with your leadership. A good leader uses intuition and observation to evaluate effort. Sometimes, a lack of effort reveals that someone isn't fully committed to the vision. Always stay alert to this, especially when building a successful program.

Their effort will show you the position they want in your life. Not their words, promises, or intentions...their effort.

Patience Is a Work in Progress

I was a program builder, a game-changer, and a difference-maker, and I knew it from day one. In past writings, I've discussed many of the qualities that helped me lead effectively, but I rarely mentioned patience. That's because it was never my strong suit. I've never been comfortable with the "wait and see" approach.

I openly admit this has been, and still is, a flaw in my character. Patience has always been a work in progress for me. There have been moments in both my personal and professional life when the Lord forced me to slow down and pay attention. I had to listen to my inner voice and lean into my faith.

My favorite verse for reassurance is **2 Corinthians 4:16-18**, a promise that good things come to those who wait on the eternal and unseen. I've had to gradually accept that some things unfold on a different timeline than my own.

The most powerful thing you can be right now is patient while things are unfolding.

Be Resilient When Confronted with Interference

Remember, everyone has someone they answer to. Most leaders must balance what's best for the children in the program with the political interests of their supervisors. And trust me, they're not always aligned.

As a leader, you must navigate this minefield while keeping your inner circle and your participants focused on the goal. True leadership requires resilience, adapting to external pressures while staying grounded in your mission.

Resilience:

The capacity of a person to maintain their core purpose and integrity in the face of dramatically changed circumstances, the ability to not only overcome setbacks but to also move forward.

Boundaries – Make Them Clear and Concise

I learned this early on as a young leader: your boundaries must be clear and concise. The world is full of people who lack filters and will consume much of your time if given the chance.

Even with boundaries in place, it helps to have a gatekeeper, someone you trust to protect your time and help others respect your space. Despite your best efforts, some individuals will still act as though boundaries apply to everyone but them.

Make sure people know your door is open, but also that your time and space must be respected.

Walls keep everybody out. Boundaries teach people where the door is.

You Are NOT Their Friend

Educating and coaching young people usually take place in public settings, fields, gyms, classrooms, tracks, and courts, where most people are welcome to observe. It's important for professionals in these environments to recognize the emotional demands of their role. Kids are watching, and many will emulate you as a leader.

But they do not need you to be their friend or to hear the details of your personal life. Keep your personal life private, and avoid getting involved in their personal matters whenever possible. It's fine to be a good listener, but it is not appropriate to insert yourself into their private lives.

The only exception is if you become aware of evidence of physical or sexual abuse. In that case, you are legally obligated to report it. Be smart. Stay on your side of the line.

I keep my personal life private. So don't think you know me. You only know what I allow you to know.

Behavior and Respect

As an educational leader, I came to value the power of modeling and promoting appropriate behavior. None of us are perfect, we all make mistakes, but effort and intention matter.

One of the biggest issues in our society today is the lack of accountability among young people. If you're a young teacher or coach, it is your responsibility to demand respect and appropriate behavior from those under your influence.

Your beliefs don't make you a better person; your behavior does.

Teach Consequences

Throughout my career, I've had the privilege of working with tens of thousands of teenagers. I always encouraged them to look within themselves for strength, growth, and passion. Many were at a point in life where they were testing boundaries and exploring their future.

I felt a deep responsibility to teach them about the opportunities available in America. I wasn't talking about equality; I was talking about possibility. We live in a country where the right to choose is protected, but every choice comes with consequences.

Freedom of choice does not mean freedom from consequence. That's why most of the programs I developed included daily activities focused on decisions and their outcomes. It's one of the many benefits of extracurricular programs in our schools.

You are free to choose, but you are not free from the consequences of your choice.

Basket Your Priorities

As an administrator, athletic director, head coach, and teacher, I learned early that situations won't wait for you to be ready. They happen, and sometimes, all at once. The chaos can feel overwhelming if you let it.

That's why I believe in preparation and anticipation. If you're strong in those areas, you'll have tools ready when the chaos hits. Even then, you may still find yourself buried in urgent tasks.

Don't just react. Pause, establish your priorities, and start with the most immediate issue. Stay calm and address each task one at a time. This approach will help you manage the chaos and return to a sense of normalcy.

When you can't control what's happening, challenge yourself to control how you respond to what's happening. That's where your power is.

Control Your Mindset

As a young professional, I struggled to learn that I couldn't control what others thought, wanted, or expected. But I could control my own contributions and expectations by choosing my mindset.

To grow and succeed, I committed to developing confidence, character, and commitment. Through that growth, I was able to influence those in my circle. Professional integrity isn't automatic, it's something you earn.

You become unstoppable when you work on things people can't take away from you. Things like your mindset, character, and personality.

Stay Calm

Staying calm in high-pressure situations was one of the toughest lessons I had to learn as an educator and coach. If you're new to the profession, know this: you will be tested by parents, staff, and participants.

A large part of your responsibility is to teach and model character, which means doing the right thing in difficult moments, not the easy thing. In highly confrontational situations, you must be the calm, reasonable, and caring voice in the room.

Take a deep breath. Say a short prayer. Put on your listening ears. But don't surrender common sense, because if you do, the lion will devour you.

Train your mind to be calm in every situation.

Emotional Control

I'm older now, but I used to believe that a man should never cry in front of others. As a leader, I often pushed my emotions aside to project strength and stability.

I've led thousands of young men into battles, on the field and in life, and I've experienced crushing defeats. Yet I always managed to console, encourage, and model hope. You can't inspire a fighting spirit with a bucket of tears.

Now, as I near the end of my career, I tell younger coaches that it's okay to show controlled emotion. Life has taught me that pain, fear, and relief often bring tears, and that's nothing to be ashamed of.

I've faced catastrophic health challenges, and I've learned that tears are sometimes necessary. They humble you and remind you of your humanity. God listens to those who seek Him. Let go of pride and allow your emotions to catch up.

But there was no need to be ashamed of tears, for tears bore witness that a man had the greatest of courage, the courage to suffer.

- Viktor E. Frankl

Adversity – Take a Pause

Early in my career, I realized that negative issues arise regularly. Reacting impulsively rarely helps. A good leader learns to pause and think before making a decision.

It's easy to let negativity overshadow all the good in your program. But your faith and poise can help you maintain perspective. The Lord promises wisdom to those who ask — James 1:5 — and offers strength through faith. Pause. Reflect. Lead.

Positive people also have negative thoughts. They just don't let it control them.

Defeat and Disappointment

Everyone falls. Everyone fails. No one is perfect, and God never expected us to be. Adversity, defeat, and disappointment are part of life.

As a leader, how you respond to those moments matters. You must feel the hurt your players and staff are feeling. Acknowledge it, and then shift the focus to the progress that has been made.

I've seen tough, grown men, some of the best athletes I've coached, break down in the pain of defeat. With God's strength, I held it together. I picked them up, dusted them off, and helped them move forward. I didn't cry or wallow, I loved them through it.

Now, my wife could tell you what happened when I got home in the middle of the night. That's when the tears came. In private. Because I was their warrior.

Even wolves get broken hearts. Even warriors cry.

- *Melody Lee.*

Develop Resolution Skills

Resolution can be elusive when it comes to conflict. Over the years, I've learned that the key lies in keeping an open mind, practicing strong listening skills, maintaining clear objectives, and being willing to compromise. These are the traits that enable an objective leader to bring opposing parties together and find a solution. My advice: always remember your role and avoid becoming part of the problem.

A door is much smaller compared to the house, a lock is much smaller compared to the door, and a key is the smallest of all. But a key can open the entire house. Thus, a small and thoughtful solution can solve major problems.

The Job Is NOT About Your Beliefs

As educators, our role is to provide students and athletes with the facts and tools they need to become independent, critical thinkers. We should want them to be the masters of their own thoughts and futures.

I am deeply concerned by the growing number of educators who impose their personal political and social beliefs on students. A true professional must avoid, at all costs, injecting their personal views into the classroom or athletic environment. In fact, in some cases, educators are deliberately omitting key facts in history or literature to influence students' beliefs. This behavior is unethical and unprofessional.

If you find yourself engaging in this kind of conduct, I urge you to reconsider your chosen profession. You are doing a disservice to your community, school, and most importantly, the students you are meant to serve.

Be a free thinker and don't accept everything you hear as truth. Be critical and evaluate what you believe in.

-Aristotle

Loyalty Is a Two-Way Street

Loyalty is always a two-way street. As an educational leader, your inner staff, organization, and community depend on you to stand by and support them through thick and thin. It's equally important that you expect the same kind of loyalty in return.

Unfortunately, there will be individuals who decide that loyalty is no longer a value they want to uphold. As a leader, you must recognize this shift. When it becomes evident, encourage them to move on to an opportunity where they can be happier and more productive. Help them find a better fit if possible.

You should do everything in your power to help transition them out of the program, because the longer they stay with a negative attitude, the more likely they are to spread toxicity to others. No one wants to be around someone radiating negative energy.

If you don't know the value of loyalty, you will never understand the damage of betrayal.

Empower Your Inner Circle

This is why selecting your inner circle carefully is so important. I always appreciated being surrounded by people who made me look better than I actually was!

Thank you to all of you who were part of my inner circle at various stages of my career. Your input, dedication, and loyalty will never be forgotten. You were the best!

The next best thing to being wise oneself is to live in a circle of those who are.

Program Supporters

How do you identify a true supporter? As a leader, it's essential to assess the sincerity and cohesiveness of those around you.

The best way I've found is to observe actions, not just listen to words. I value individuals who are positive and proactive. They use encouraging words, uplifting gestures, and praise. A true supporter rolls up their sleeves and works alongside you. They stay late, help others, and advocate for your expectations.

When you find someone who consistently embodies these qualities, keep them close, and invite them into your inner circle.

Sit with people who protect your name in your absence.

Mentor and Support Your Staff Members

As an Athletic Director, I always encouraged my staff to set and pursue professional goals. Though I didn't want to lose them to other programs, I often spoke with them about new opportunities and career growth.

At one point, I held a staff meeting with 21 assistant coaches and 15 head coaches. The final item on the agenda was something I felt strongly about: professional advancement. At that time, only two of us, including myself, had earned a Master's degree.

I announced my expectation that every coach in the room would earn their Master's within two years. This was met with immediate resistance. But I assured them I would accommodate their after-school responsibilities so they could attend classes. I made it clear this was not optional, those who didn't make a genuine effort would be let go.

Two years later, all but two had earned their degree. The two who didn't, voluntarily left the staff. The rest went on to excel in school administration and counseling. Many of them eventually became leaders in their own right, captaining their own ships.

A wise man once said, "Be careful who you let on your ship, because some people will sink the whole ship just because they can't be the captain."

Understand the Progression of Talent

This is excellent coaching advice from Coach Saban: If you're a young coach, understand the progression of talent on your team.

You'll have players with average knowledge and skill. You and your assistants will spend much of the season helping them grow. Then you'll have players with above-average skills and understanding. These individuals can help you bring the average players along, improving everyone's performance in the process.

These two groups will likely make up the majority of your team. Their growing confidence and ability will elevate the entire program.

Finally, you'll have a few highly gifted athletes. These are your potential leaders. Your job is to fine-tune their talents and show appreciation for their contributions, while also teaching them humility and gratitude for being part of the team.

As the season progresses, you'll witness a bond of unity and a shared expectation of success. Remember, it's not where you start, but how far you grow. That mindset leads to ultimate achievement.

Average players want to be left alone. Good players want to be coached. Great players want to be told the truth.

Lean on Your Will and Expectations

As a professional educator, I never accepted the words *cannot, will not, should not,* or *I don't know how.* Everyone believes they have limits, but the key to leadership is showing a level of confidence and commitment that spills over to everyone around you, staff, parents, and students.

Many people remain confined to their comfort zones. As a change agent, you must use your will and expectations to inspire others to step beyond those boundaries. Push them to work harder, move forward, and tear down walls of resistance.

Be aware: this work can be draining. That's why you must give God the glory and pray for strength — 1 Peter 1:13.

Whatever you do, never let anyone or anything impede your progress. Stay focused, and keep moving forward.

People who say it cannot be done should not interrupt those who are doing it.

Success Is Earned – Not a Given Right

Good coaches watch and grade film, critique performances, and push hard in practice. It's something many parents don't fully understand. A player earns playing time through performance. Repeated mistakes, mental or physical, hurt the team and can affect the outcome of a game.

Coaches are paid to assemble a team, define each player's role, share their knowledge of the game, and positively influence players and fellow coaches. But let's not pretend, coaches are also expected to win. And sometimes, even that's not enough to keep the job.

I don't have a problem with high expectations. My concern lies with participation trophies and ribbons. When parents and communities reward mere presence, it sends the wrong message. Kids, especially the young, need to understand that hard work and determination are what lead to success.

If they grow up thinking things will just be handed to them, we risk raising a generation that doesn't understand the value of effort and accomplishment.

Lead From Within

To all young educators: be your authentic self. Nobody's perfect. We all make mistakes.

When you work with other people's children, sincerity, commitment, and an open mind is non-negotiable. And perhaps the most essential quality of all is respect. Kids come in all shapes, sizes, and intellectual abilities, but they all have a built-in honesty meter.

They can sense insecurity, vulnerability, and dishonesty from a mile away. You have to be real with them. Be the genuine article.

This authenticity gives you an edge, because it opens the door to a relationship built on mutual respect. I began each school year with this understanding. Eventually, the kids came to see that respect was a two-way street. And when they showed us their true selves, I adjusted my perception.

Many of them came to realize I wasn't vulnerable at all, and that there were consequences for attitude and misbehavior.

If you get the different me,
that means I saw the real you.

Believe That You Can Be the Difference

Much of your success will depend on your mindset. You must believe that you can make a difference. Let your enthusiasm and energy shine through.

I can't count how many times I got into trouble for moving forward without hesitation. I never saw much value in waiting for permission, because you can always ask for forgiveness later.

Doing something positive is always better than making excuses for what wasn't done.

If it's important to you, you'll find a way. If not, you'll find an excuse.

Inspirational Leader for All

As an educational leader, I made it my mission to build genuine relationships. Every staff member, student, and athlete played a role in our collective progress.

Make the effort to truly get to know those you serve. Learn what stirs their hearts and fuels their spirits. Gather your thoughts and your vision, then set out to inspire.

Let every individual know how important they are. Encourage them to follow. You won't inspire everyone, but you can be a source of inspiration for all.

The most important thing is to try to inspire people so that they can be great in whatever they want to do.

Passion for the Game

What is passion for the game? It's the desire to contribute as a player, a teammate, and a student of the sport.

When you overcome fear and hesitation, you give yourself a chance to be your best. Replace hesitation with performance.

That transformation only comes through hard work, commitment, and dedication. If you never swing the bat, you'll never hit the ball.

We change in a positive way when our love for it is greater than the fear of it.

Life Lessons from the Game

I fell in love with football at a young age. I played Pee Wee through sixth grade, then continued in junior high and high school. I became one of the best players in my small town and county.

Later, I played small college football while pursuing my degree. When choosing my college major, I knew I wanted to become a teacher and football coach. I gave the decision careful thought, but in the end, my heart knew: I wanted to share my passion for the game with the next generation.

I've often been asked why it was so important to me. My answer has always been the same:

Football, and athletics as a whole, offers countless lessons and opportunities for young people to develop the tools they need to succeed in life.

Football life lessons

1. *You are part of something bigger than yourself.*
2. *You play how you practice. Practice hard.*
3. *Every inch of progress gets you closer to the goal.*
4. *Keep your eye on the goal.*
5. *Celebrate the wins.*
6. *Believe in yourself.*
7. *Learn from losses.*
8. *Being disciplined pays off.*
9. *Winning requires teamwork.*
10. *Work hard and play smart.*

Recognize Your Superpower

We each have our own unique superpower. Mine has always been a dynamic inner voice that guides me through troubled waters. If you know me well, you can likely testify to my strong will and relentless drive to move forward. There is a fighting spirit within me, persistent and determined, that has carried me through difficult times. But this same trait can be a disadvantage when the moment calls for stillness, understanding, and acceptance. Letting go, whether after the passing of a friend or when facing a necessary goodbye as life shifts toward a new challenge, requires a gentler strength. These moments are especially hard for me, because letting go is a very different act than fighting to hold on.

Maybe your superpower is refusing to give up, even on your weakest days when you feel you're not enough.

-Christy Ann Martine

INNER VOICE

Rely on Your Inner Spirit

I often speak about our inner spirit, our inner voice. It's quite literally God-given. After forming the physical body, God breathed into it and created the soul — **Genesis 2:7.** This divine breath gave us spiritual awareness. I believe every person has the free will to tune into that voice at any moment.

In my roles as an administrator, teacher, and coach, I've experienced my share of chaotic, stressful days. If you're still reading, you've likely had them too. Early in my career, I battled through those days without truly listening to my inner voice, and it took a toll on my health and well-being. Eventually, I reached a breaking point, and that's when God stepped in to get my attention. His message was clear: *Pay attention and listen. I will provide you with strength and guidance* — **Joshua 1:9.**

Since then, I've developed a personal strategy for handling stress: take a few deep breaths, say a short prayer for strength, listen closely, set priorities, and make decisions with grace. When the storm passes, I close my eyes and offer a prayer of gratitude. Everyone faces difficult days. What matters is having a plan and moving through them with faith and confidence.

The old soul that dwells at the core of each person has a tolerance for chaos and an instinct for survival.

Inner Voice – Trust Your Intuition

Most people refer to intuition as a gut feeling, but I believe it's much deeper than that, more spiritual in nature. As educators, we spend a great deal of time teaching right from wrong, and the importance of doing the right thing. But intuition isn't just about morality, it's the voice of the soul. It's God's way of nudging us to pay attention. That little spark of concern, that quick reflection, often offers valuable insight. We all have the choice to listen to it or not. But over time, we can learn to recognize and honor it more consistently.

Your intuition is the most honest friend that you will ever have.

Your Inner Voice Counts

This inner voice, the one I've come to trust deeply, is your connection to your soul. Learn to hear it. Let it guide your responses. A strong leader is one who develops this skill instead of ignoring it. We've all seen leaders who react without thinking, and we know how much can go wrong in that approach. The more you learn to pause and truly listen, the more effectively you can manage your daily responsibilities, and the smoother life tends to flow.

Between stimulus and response, there is a space. In that space is our power to choose our response. In our response lies our growth and our freedom.

-VIKTOR E. FRANKL

Have a Soulful Inner Voice

This concept is somewhat new to me, having what some might call a "dope soul." But I'm beginning to understand what it means. Each of us is born with unique gifts, breathed into us by God — Genesis 2:7. Our soul is the essence of who we are: our identity, our personality, our perceptions, and reflections. These soulful traits shape our faith, our purpose, and our calling, not just in life, but beyond. When we nurture this part of ourselves, we begin to recognize our true purpose. For me, that purpose is found in working with, encouraging, and building meaningful relationships with the children I've been privileged to influence.

Built, not bought. Earned, not given. Hustled, not handed. Rare, not average.

Let Your Inner Voice Be Your Guide

This topic hits close to home for me. It helps explain the struggles I've encountered throughout my career. I'm not sure I've always been wise, but I've grown from experience. In my younger years, I was more naïve, but even then, I felt called to bring light into darkness. That strength, that inner glow of faith, helped me navigate through obstacles and uncertainty.

If I could leave one piece of advice for a young educator, it would be this: *Lean on your inner voice and spirit. Let them guide you.* And may God bless you; you've chosen a challenging, but deeply rewarding, path.

I am just an old wandering soul. So, don't blame me for the mischief that I keep getting myself into as wise as the oaks and as naive as the moon I am, Always seeking light in the dark and love in the ruins.

Let Your Inner Voice Burn Brightly

Some people are naturally calm and easygoing. That's never been me! Those who know me well will tell you I'm anything but complacent. Some folks believe in fate, that things just happen, regardless of their actions. I'm not one of them. I believe in preparation, willpower, independence, and personal responsibility.

If you want to succeed, your work ethic, integrity, character, and faith must come together to form a powerful force. These qualities are what keep my inner voice burning bright. Be brave. Reflect on what fuels your spirit, and let it blaze!

I go to war every day for my loves, for my life, my warrior heart floods my veins with unyielding fight
giving up is truly not in my blood.

A.   Shea

The Light of Your Inner Spirit

Life is incredibly short. Over the years, I've learned that God has a clear purpose for each of us. If you listen closely to your inner voice, you'll notice that He is constantly providing opportunities to fulfill that purpose. Sometimes, He even works through others, blessing you with opportunities sparked by their own inner spirit.

As an effective leader, you must believe that others have the ability to brighten the light within you, especially in moments of need. No one truly succeeds alone. We all need spiritual support. As you focus on building something meaningful, whether a program, a team, or a community, remember to stay grounded and listen to that inner voice.

There will always be a reason why you meet people. Either you need them to change your life, or you're the one that will change theirs.

Cultivate Your Inner Voice

As an educational leader for 40 years, I hope I've encouraged others to find and nurture the voice within themselves. I challenge each of you to instill this same awareness and confidence in your children and grandchildren. When we pass it forward, we help shape an entire generation.

The one thing that you have that nobody else has is you. Your voice, your mind, your story, your vision. So. write and draw and build and play and dance and live as only you can:

- Neil Gaiman

Be Yourself, Trust Your Inner Voice

To all the young professional educators who follow my writing: don't be afraid to be yourself. Authenticity is key when working with other people's children. I've always been willful, deliberate, confident, caring, and committed. I saw my role as one of motivating, leading, and influencing those within my reach. I was outspoken and held high expectations, but always with a spirit of goodwill.

Don't be afraid to listen to and rely on your inner voice and spirit. *"God will reward each of us according to what we have done"* — **Romans 2:6.**

I choose to live by choice, not by chance; to make changes, not excuses; to be motivated, not manipulated; to be useful, not used; to excel, not to compete. I choose self-esteem, not self-pity. I choose to listen to my inner voice, not the random opinion of others. I choose to be me.

Lead With Your Inner Spirit

This message reflects the spirit I brought to working with the young people in our programs. There was never any doubt why I devoted so much time and effort, it was for their success. I hoped to instill work ethic, self-confidence, achievement, and a positive outlook that would serve them for life.

Of the thousands I was blessed to influence, many have gone on to enjoy fulfilling careers, earn an education, and raise families. I can't speak for all of them, but I know many are out there making a difference. To each of you, I say congratulations!

The reward of our work is not what we get, but what we become.

- Paulo Coelho

Depend on Your Inner Strength

The illustration below perfectly captures the inner strength and spiritual awareness that have sustained me. As a leader and advocate for cultural change, I've faced many challenges that tested my professionalism, character, and credibility.

Yet somehow, I often managed to stay calm and composed. I once had a guidance counselor ask, "How do you stay so together and calm in the face of adversity?" She was referring to a heartbreaking situation in which I had to address our team about the death of one of their teammates and his parents.

I told her, "Cindy, my faith and spiritual strength are all I have, and they've guided me with unwavering devotion." I may be a secular man outwardly, but I carry a deeply spiritual heart. That night, I went home, cried myself to sleep, and prayed, for understanding and obedience.

Do not be afraid. Do not be discouraged. For the Lord your God will be with you wherever you go.

Be Inwardly Spiritual

I've shared often about the spirit within me and the importance of listening to your inner voice. My leadership style has been outwardly secular but inwardly spiritual. I don't wear my faith on my sleeve, but I try to live it through my actions.

God's love and commitment have been a source of strength through adversity. If you know me, you know I care deeply and reach out often. If you want to be a great leader, you must find and listen to your spiritual inner voice.

The Holy Spirit's Voice is as loud as your willingness to listen.

A Course in Miracles, T-8 VIIL8:5

Inner Voice - Angels Are Among Us

I truly believe angels walk among us. While the practical side of me might dismiss it, my spiritual inner voice, given by the Lord, assures me they are real. I've had moments when I *knew* I was in the presence of angels, guiding me through some of life's hardest moments.

Those who know me trust my judgment. And I'm telling you, my angels came at just the right times, lifting my spirits, healing my heart. I'm humbled and grateful for their presence.

In return, I try to pay it forward. I minister quietly to those experiencing grief, illness, trauma, divorce, anxiety, and more. I show up unannounced, listen, and offer comfort from my soul. You might say I'm a lighthouse; a beacon of the blessings God has given me.

The ones who sit with and listen to the fallen.

The ones who cheer on and the people succeeding. The ones who show up with a smile and mean it. The ones who look for the lost. remember the forgotten, and love with their whole soul. These are lighthouses shining all over the planet, in the shape of human beings.

-Stacie Martin

Daily Devotion and Quiet Time

The illustration below reflects lessons I learned in the latter part of my career. But they apply to every profession. The five P's of daily success help balance work and life:

1. **Prayer**

2. **Priorities**

3. **Peace**

4. **Purpose**

5. **Patience**

These principles help keep your inner voice strong and bright. I often write about the inner voice because it needs your attention and care. I recommend a little daily devotion and quiet time. I tend to reflect late at night before bed, but whatever time works for you, don't neglect it. Your faith and strength depend on it.

Stay on your Ps.

Prayer. Priorities. Peace. Purpose. Patience.

Stay Calm, Listen to Your Inner Voice

As an administrator, head coach, and teacher, I've faced countless situations that required calm under pressure. I can recall many times when I felt turmoil, anger, and even resentment bubbling up inside.

The illustration below captures that frustration well. *Lol!* But through it all, I relied on divine guidance to still my heart and mind.

"Those who control their anger have great understanding; those with a hasty temper will make mistakes." —**Proverbs 14:29**

This verse has helped me through many tense moments. Sometimes it feels impossible to stay calm, but I still take a deep breath and try to listen to my inner voice.

I may look calm but in my head
I've slapped you 3 times.